W9-ARP-927

HYPERION

ESPN
BOOKS

BY CHARLES HIRSHBERG

FOREWORD BY CHRIS BERMAN

EDITOR: **Jay Lovinger**
DESIGN DIRECTOR: **Walter Bernard**
ART DIRECTOR: **Julia Zichello**
PHOTO EDITOR: **Dot McMahon**
ASSISTANT PHOTO EDITOR: **Mary Jane Kinney**
SENIOR WRITER (lists): **Jeff Merron**
RESEARCH: **Gueorgui Milkov**

Copyright© 2004 ESPN, Inc.
All rights reserved. No part of this book may be
used or reproduced in any manner whatsoever
without the written permission of the Publisher.
Printed in the United States of America.
For information address Hyperion,
77 West 66th Street, New York, New York
10023-6298.
ISBN: 1-4013-3704-X

Hyperion books are available for special promo-
tions and premiums. For details contact Michael
Rentas, Manager, Inventory and Premium Sales,
Hyperion, 77 West 66th Street, 11th floor,
New York, New York 10023, or call 212-456-0133.

First Edition
10 9 8 7 6 5 4 3 2 1

To Richard I. Hirshberg—Ohio Conference track-and-field star, decorated veteran of World War II, anthropologist, complex systems analyst, outdoorsman, and friend to the whole canine nation—this book is lovingly dedicated.

Also, to my brother Matt, who convinced me when I was seven that playing catch with him would be more fun than sitting on top of the fence, flirting with the girl next door. Matt reversed his opinion on this some years later; and yet, remarkably, he was right both times. My big brother is *always* right.

—*Charles Hirshberg*

Ozzie Smith's exuberant flip as he comes on the field at the start of a playoff game against the Giants, October 7, 1987

Back
Back
Back
Back
Back!

SEPTEMBER 7, 1979. ESPN WAS BORN. History now tells us that the television sports landscape was forever changed that Friday. Funny, though; those of us who worked at ESPN back in the fall of 1979 and the beginning of the 1980s weren't so sure.

The only landscape we were changing was the quagmire outside of our one building on Middle Street in bucolic Bristol, Connecticut. It went from mud that Noah's Ark fall to frozen mud that New England winter. We were told one day it would be our parking lot. Outsiders thought that in a few years ESPN, as an entity, might become a parking lot.

Now, of course, it's 25 years later. We don't have enough parking lots for our growing army of employees. Landscapers are at work planting trees and shrubs around our expanding "campus." Inside, on a nightly basis, difficult sports television decisions are being made . . . for *SportsCenter, NFL Primetime*, and a gaggle of other shows. How can we fit all these highlights into an hour show?

If they only knew.

Back in the early days, we were thrilled to have any "pictures" to show. Of course, if you were one of the lucky ones to have cable TV, or even know what cable TV was, you could turn on ESPN and see our picture. We did *SportsCenter* three times a night—in the early evening, at 11 eastern, and then at 2:20 or 3 A.M. They were, for the most part, half-hour shows in the very beginning, but with one major difference from what you see now: There were very few highlights.

How could that be? Think of TV back then—over-the-air and fledgling cable. Not many games were on. You couldn't look to the sky to grab action from another coast, because games weren't broadcast on "the bird."

By being in Connecticut, we actually got a break. We're located between New York and Boston, which meant we could record the over-the-air broadcasts of the teams from both cities. That meant the Yankees, Mets, and Red Sox . . . and whoever they were playing. That meant the Giants, Jets and Patriots, and the national doubleheader game . . . say, the Cowboys hosting the Redskins, or the Raiders hosting the Chiefs. That meant the Knicks, Nets and Celtics in basketball . . . and in hockey, the Rangers, Islanders, Bruins and our own Hartford Whalers. The Devils weren't in New Jersey yet.

Occasionally, we'd arrange for tapes to be driven up from Philadelphia, and it was a good year for that, because the Phillies, Eagles, 76ers and Flyers would all play in the championship round of their sports. Then, for true out-of-town games, we'd get previous-day tapes flown in to the airport in Hartford. We used to say: "If the planes are landing at Bradley International, we'll have yesterday's news tonight." And we were thrilled to have it.

True, there were large pockets of the country we were missing. But we had more than anyone else. Now came the fun part—showing America what actually happened in a game.

The beauty was, we had a blank canvas. Those 20- or 30-second clips you'd see on your local 3½-minute sportscast became a minute, or a minute and a half—maybe more. It was storytelling, TV-style, and in the sports business, we felt like we were inventors, like Edison with the lightbulb or Ford with the mass-produced car.

Soon, we stopped relying so much on TV antennas, cars and planes. Games were on TV in midweek—on the satellite—and we could pull them all in. Those of us who worked from 8 P.M. till 4 A.M., on the overnight *SportsCenter* that eventually would re-air in the morning, had it best. On, say, a Tuesday night, we saw everything that was on TV. Pro and college. East Coast . . . central time zone . . . the Rockies . . . the West Coast. The 2:30 A.M. *SportsCenter* was tomorrow's sports section, only with pictures and words. It was a delight to put together, and a delight to present.

The highlight became the game story. We showed how a game was won, or lost—who were the stars, or goats—and while the pictures were playing, we could squeeze in details like statistics, and narrate the sequences in our own style. The key, in one man's opinion, was to do them as if you were watching them live, because, after all, the viewers didn't know who won until you told them and showed them.

ESPN viewers were, and always will be, sports fans. If you could take them to 10 baseball games on a given night, they'd be in heaven. So why not try? If you could speak to your viewers as if you were in the stadium seat next to them, so much the better. So why not do it?

Sports fans are the most loyal people we know. Loyal to their team, or town, or alma mater. Loyal to their favorite players, or particular sport. Did we mention knowledgeable? In time, they have become loyal to ESPN, and it's that relationship that we "old-timers" cherish the most. There's a trust factor that goes both ways.

Times have changed, the TV business has changed . . . so, too, has our presentation of the sports news. Information is available to all at the touch of a button . . . or click of a mouse. But to the sports fans, showing and telling them why a team won and why a team lost remains paramount.

Which is why that remains ESPN's most important task—presenting the sports with information, enthusiasm, intelligence and entertainment, and probably in that order. I don't see that ever changing. If it does, you'd better let me know about it—and I promise to take care of it right away.

—*Chris Berman*

A Catalogue of Wonders

'M CERTAINLY NOT A FANATIC OR ANYTHING LIKE THAT," BASEBALL MANAGER and ethicist Sparky Anderson once told ESPN. "But I *do* believe we've got a Big Guy. And I believe the Big Guy made all of us. He made the grass, the water, the rocks—everything. And if He did that, then He meant for all of us to be the same. . . . How can anybody be better than somebody else? The only thing you can be is *more fortunate*."

To put it another way, a large part of being good involves being the recipient of a good deal of good fortune. And for the last 25 years, ESPN has been the most fortunate network in America. Oh, sure, the place is the product of inspiration, exertion and teamwork. But all of those things are requirements for success, not prescriptions for it. Indeed, any blessing collected without inspiration, exertion and teamwork can't be called "success" in any meaningful sense of the word. Rather, it's the sort of thing that happens to kids whom we call "spoiled" or to adults whom we call "team owners."

None of which detracts from the immense creativity, and even flashes of genius, described hereafter in this book. But if ESPN has revolutionized not only sports broadcasting, but the American experience of sports itself—and it has—it didn't do so by means of some ingenious master plan. The wonderful truth is, no one in their wildest imaginings predicted that ESPN would ever accomplish what it has in the last quarter century. Not its brilliant founder Bill Rasmussen, who would have been just as happy building a TV network for sports-loving alumni of the University of Connecticut (for that was his original idea). Not the corporate moneybags from Getty Oil who backed Rasmussen, made millions of bucks off the venture and then cashed out, leaving others to make billions. And, for goodness sake, not the anchors. Cast them away on a desert island and ESPN's anchors would put on a special Desert Island Edition of *SportsCenter* for the seagulls, because that is what they were born to do. Not that they're selfless, mind you; they're as fond of money as you or I. But they love sports even more.

Falling Short
The agony of defeat comes in many flavors. To the Tennessee Titans, it tasted like a mouthful of air, just shy of the end zone. To a Milwaukee sausage, it tasted like a mouthful of dirt.

How did it happen? Twenty-five years ago, Americans got most of their sports news from the newspaper (remember the "newspaper"?), and from a two-to-three-minute wrap-up at the very end of the 11 o'clock news. Almost all of that news was local and secondhand. Hard-core sports fans subscribed to *Sports Illustrated* and crazed sports junkies subscribed to *The Sporting News*, and it cannot be said that many Americans were unhappy with the state of affairs. There was certainly no Million Sports Fan March to demand better sports reporting. Nonetheless, ESPN provided it. And it did so by adopting, and perfecting, an underutilized, unappreciated method of communication: the sports highlight.

Picture Perfect
All great high-lights tell a story. It might be a story about (clockwise from top left) breaking an unbreakable deadlock, making an impossible comeback, getting nailed when you least expect it, or eating on the job.

Human beings," wrote Harvard paleontologist and sports fan Stephen Jay Gould, "are pattern-seeking, story-telling creatures," and ESPN has made highlights the primary means by which the patterns and stories of sports are revealed. It's a perfect medium for modern America, with its Incredible Shrinking Attention Span and its cut-to-the-chase-and-show-me-what-you-got values. A good highlight is at once a poetic distillation of athleticism and a carnival barker's holler for your attention, a shameless effort to keep you from pressing that damned remote.

So this book, ostensibly about ESPN, is really about highlights—their history, their impact and their implications. It is not so much a celebration of the highlight as a catalogue of wonder. "When you think you've seen something that you'll never see again," Sparky Anderson says of sports, "get ready. You're gonna see something better." That is also a perfect description of what ESPN highlights have shown us over the last 25 years. The proof is on your TV screen and in these pages.

—*Charles Hirshberg*

CHAPTER 1

Let There Be Highlights

SPORTS HIGHLIGHTS ARE OLDER THAN SPORTS. This is no hyperbole, for the practice of recording heroic feats of athleticism goes back tens of thousands of years, at least to the Paleolithic period, or Old Stone Age. Obviously, there were no sports in those days, as we think of them—no baseball, no miniature golf. There were, however, heroic hunters, the likes of which we shall never see again.

Our prehistoric ancestors hunted for survival, but archaeologists report that they were both ingeniously creative and ferociously competitive in their approach. Since creativity and competition are precisely the elements through which athletics would eventually be rendered into sports, it's safe to say that hunting was both a nascent sport and the Mother of All Sports to Come. The life of a Stone Age hunter was nasty, brutish and short, but it was also blessed with occasional transcendent moments, and from those moments arose primeval religion, art . . . and sports highlights.

The earliest known highlight appears to have been produced about 16,000 years ago in, of all places, France. (Rest assured, France has changed considerably since the Paleolithic Age.) The details of exactly what happened are murky, but it may have gone something like this: One day, a band of hunters set out from their cave dwellings near the present-day

Win, or be dead A hunting scene painted on a cave wall near Lascaux, France, 16,000 years ago may be the world's oldest known sports highlight.

"SPORTS GUYS SAY THE DARNEDEST THINGS"

town of Lascaux in search of game. Luck was with them, or so it seemed, for they came upon a monstrous bison. Not one of the 1,000-pound American bison that Buffalo Bill Cody was so proud of a-shootin' and a-skinnin', but a much larger species, now extinct. It would have taken a ridiculous amount of courage for a lone man to confront such a beast with the only weapons a Stone Age hunter could call upon—a spear or an ax. Nonetheless, one of the hunters found that courage and managed to slice open the creature's underbelly, sending its intestines spilling out onto the ground. At this point, it's likely that one cave man turned to another and shouted essentially the same thing that Jack Buck shouted into his CBS Radio microphone when a hobbled Kirk Gibson belted his impossible game-winning homer off Dennis Eckersley in Game 1 of the 1988 World Series: "I don't believe what I just saw!"

The dying bison was understandably irritated and took revenge, killing the hunter with its mighty horns. But a bison carcass that size must have kept the grateful Lascaux cave community well fed for quite some time, and they decided that the hunter's deed was too fine to pass unremembered.

All of this is speculation; we will never know exactly what happened, but it doesn't matter. What *does* matter is that, 16,000 years ago on the wall of a Lascaux cave now known as "The Shaft of the Dead Man," a dramatic scene was painted for posterity. The magnificent bison is shown dragging its innards along the ground, horns poised threateningly over the doomed hunter, who falls backward with his arms splayed helplessly at his sides. And as a tribute to the hunter's great manliness, the artist has thoughtfully endowed him with a pronounced male organ. (What athlete of today wouldn't appreciate being depicted the same way on his Hall of Fame plaque?) This highlight is a vivid reminder that, for most of human history, athletic ability was not about games; it was the difference between survival and death. No wonder, even as civilizations developed, and with them, herding and agriculture, which made hunting far less important, people continued to revere athletic heroism, to celebrate it in contests of sport—and to preserve, in art and in memory, those spectacular moments when they could not believe what they had just seen.

The ancient Greeks had a word for such moments: *arete*. It's an untranslatable word—not even the Greeks could agree

"'Marvelous Marvin' and 'Sugar Ray'? Sounds like a pillow fight between a hairdresser and an interior decorator."
—Comedian Jan Murray

on what it meant. *Arete* was a call to perfection that was said to smolder in the soul of every Greek. But its most glorious fulfillment occurred in athletic triumph, when *arete* became a fire that lit up all the noble virtues of the ancient world: not just physical power, but courage, prowess and excellence itself. At such moments, even the gods, those moody, tantrum-throwing, thunderbolt-hurling tyrants, would look down on the athlete with grudging admiration. One of them would bestow kudos, a grant of temporary invincibility that would protect the athlete even in time of war—for it was now war, far more than hunting, that was the force behind athletic competition. Athletes who won repeatedly were thus considered semidivine, and a few even came to be worshiped as gods.

> "You'd think he **discovered**
> The **cure** for **cancer**
> or something."
> —Candy Davis, wife of Royals reliever
> Mark, after her husband signed a 4-year,
> $13 million contract

Arete, or something very much like it, lies at the heart of just about every great sports highlight of our time: Ali flattening Liston, Bobby Thomson winning the pennant with a single stroke, Secretariat thundering to Triple Crown victory in the Belmont Stakes by 31 lengths. And did any Greek athlete boast more *arete* than Michael Jordan, who, even in this far more secular age, came to be worshiped as semidivine throughout much of the world?

Wrestlemania *Milo of ancient Greece, the original human highlight, would wrestle anything, and eat it, too.*

That's not a rhetorical question. I really wanted to know, and given the kinship between the Greeks and ourselves in matters of sport, I figured the ancients must have recorded the deeds of their greatest champions in roughly the same way we do (minus the videotape). After all, classical archaeologist Stephen G. Miller writes that "nearly every aspect of athletics we know today," including a lucrative sports entertainment industry, "existed already in that distant but kindred land." Surely, there must have been some sort of Panhellenic *SportsCenter* where the deeds of great athletes were recounted and relived.

But apparently there wasn't. The relatively few surviving stories about Greek sporting events tend to be pretty quirky. A great wrestler named Milo—whose daily training diet was said to consist of 40 pounds of bread and meat and eight quarts of wine—once hoisted a bull onto his shoulders and trotted around the Olympic stadium, showing off for the fans. Then he butchered the poor creature and ate it, all by himself in a single day. A Corinthian racehorse named Breeze once threw her rider, but raced on until she crossed the finish line and "recognized her victory." The Greeks were so delighted with Breeze's *arete* that they built a statue in her honor. Finally, a widow named Kallipateira longed to see her son, Peisirodos, compete in the Olympics, but women were barred from the stadium. Kallipateira gained entry by disguising herself as her son's coach, but she became so exuberant when he won, she leapt high in the air and "inadvertently exposed herself." Thenceforth, it was decreed that all coaches, like all contestants, would be required to strip naked before entering the stadium.

This is the sort of stuff *SportsCenter* uses for laughs, like streakers at Wimbledon or the Milwaukee Brewers sausage races. In lieu of highlights, the *arete* of a Greek athlete was usually commemorated with a statue, or with a specially commissioned ode. Pindar was a poet of the 5th century B.C. who became famous for recording the triumphs of sports celebrities, but his works are remarkably short on details. "He has won six times at Pellana and Aegina," reads a typical verse in praise of a pugilist named Diagoras. "O, Father Zeus . . . give honor to his now famous *arete* in boxing!" Pindar's focus, says Paul Christesen, a professor of Greek history at Dartmouth College, reflects the Greek attitude that it mattered only whether you won or lost, not how you played the game.

But though the ancestors of today's highlights are not to be found in the pious odes of Pindar, or at the base of any statue, they existed in ancient Greece nonetheless.

Hercules and Theseus were, of course, two mythic figures, each commanded by the gods to complete a series of arduous labors, by which they attained immortality. They were also Greece's greatest sports heroes. Theseus, for instance, was forced to fight King Cercyon, a tyrant who would wrestle, and

Say hey, Zeus *The Greeks called it* arete— *athletic triumph so transcendent, even the gods were impressed. Arete* is *difficult to define, but you know it when you see it, by how it makes you feel—roughly, the way Willie Mays made you feel when he robbed Cleveland's Vic Wertz in the first game of the '54 World Series.*

then kill, any Greek who ventured into his realm. But "Theseus lifted him up by the knees and, to the delight of Demeter [Goddess of Agriculture], who witnessed the struggle, dashed him headlong to the ground," records Robert Graves. "Cercyon's death was instantaneous. Theseus did not trust to strength so much as skill, for he had invented the art of wrestling."

Artistic representations of the same scene are startlingly realistic. If *SportsCenter* had covered Theseus's battle with Cercyon, the highlights would probably have looked a lot like one of the famous "red figure" vase paintings of the legend. "The ancient Greeks thought much more metaphorically than we tend to do," explains Christesen, "so these mythological scenes are highlight reels of sorts." In addition, "artists developed a 'look' for Theseus that was recognizable to Athenians." Like highlight reels, they were seen everywhere, carved on the sides of temples, painted on every sort of crockery, and burned into every child's imagination from the moment he or she was capable of understanding them. "And though Theseus was believed to be different from the 'average' Greek in a variety of ways," says Christesen, "there was also at least a theoretical possibility that anyone could follow his path and become semi-divine."

It is no accident that *SportsCenter*'s highlights have far more in common with the ever-powerful mythology of ancient Greece than with its stale athletic records. For us, as for the ancients, the value of spectator sports lies in the wonder inspired by each new act of *arete* and the mythology that surrounds our athletic heroes.

S ports fans of a certain age love to complain that sports ain't what they used to be because of the damn media. Back in the day, they'll tell you (if you let them), athletes trained in the wholesome haven of the YMCA, drank nothing stronger than RC Cola and thought that sex was the number that came after five. Then along came TV, with its lewd commercials and its preposterous hype, and Howard Cosell talking through his damn nose. Then the final insult: cable. You never had to pay for Russ Hodges or Vin Scully. Why in hell should you have to pay for Dan Patrick and Stuart Scott? Look at sports today: salaries and egos—through the

"**Sly has some personal problems.** There's been a **slight death** in the family."
—The Knicks' Sly Williams, trying to pass himself off as his brother, explaining on the phone why he missed a workout

Godfather of hype Pindar (522-443 B.C.), poet and publicist for jocks of old.

19

"This is Athenian SportsCenter"
A typical ancient vase painting of Theseus's legendary victory over Cercyon is meticulously realistic. Had ESPN covered the ancient Olympics, highlights of the wrestling events would probably have looked essentially the same.

roof. Teamwork and sportsmanship—down the toilet. Nobody respects their sport anymore; everybody just wants to watch themselves on *SportsCenter*.

There's some truth in this rant. But the deeper truth is, American sports and American media have been joined at the hip for more than a century. It's no coincidence that many of the sports we love best—football, baseball, basketball—didn't even exist in their present form until after the Civil War, when technology made mass media possible. In the 1840s, a game of "football" played in a Maine village may have been completely different from a game of the same name played on a Delaware farm. It was media that got everyone playing by the same rules; media that made baseball our national game and football a Thanksgiving Day spectacle; media that created the first national sports heroes; and media that turned hordes of curious fans into communities with shared experiences.

Today's sports highlight is a culmination of this long, close relationship between sports and media. It is a method of storytelling that no one invented. Like homo sapiens, it evolved from a long series of random accidents, unsought opportunities and an occasional stroke of inspiration.

One day in 1867, the newspaper editors and telegraph operators of Philadelphia were shocked to find their offices besieged by crowds of people panting for news. Not that such crowds were unprecedented: During the recent Civil War, Philadelphians had often assembled in such places, with fear and trembling, to learn the fates of loved ones in battle. But these Philadelphians were baseball fans, inquiring, with fear and trembling, about the fate of the Athletics, who had traveled to Morrisania (a neighborhood in the Bronx) to battle the Unions. University of Nebraska historian Benjamin Rader, author of *American Sports*, reckons this event was one of the first symptoms of the country's new, insatiable appetite for sports news—an appetite that has grown steadily (except for interruptions from the occasional world war) ever since.

The clamor for sports news caught the 19th-century media completely by surprise. There was nothing remotely resembling a "sports section" in the newspapers of the time, and very few periodicals devoted to sports—just three in the early 1840s. But that number would increase sixteenfold by the end of the century. The new sports media got off to a rocky start, though, because reporting sports proved to be unlike reporting anything else.

To begin with, the rules of baseball, and especially football, were still works in progress, and ordinary beat reporters didn't understand them very well. Nineteenth-century football coverage has been analyzed in great detail by Michael Oriard, a former offensive lineman for the Kansas City Chiefs and now an English professor at Oregon State specializing in rhetoric. In the 1870s, he says, reporters focused mostly on "football as a spectacle, or social event." A representative article from the *Portland Oregonian* described "the huge audience" at a football game, marveling that the "ladies" seemed to take "an equal interest in the contest," and that the noise of cheering was "frightful." At the conclusion of this game, the crowd "swarmed all over the field in the wildest excitement, sweeping fences and ropes before them," and carrying the players

> **"I'm trying not to put too much pressure on myself, but I think I'm overcompensating. I'm putting too much pressure on myself not to put too much pressure on myself."**
> —Dann Bilardello, Pirates catcher

Stuff of legends Some might call Ali our Theseus, but Ali would probably reply that Theseus was the Greek version of himself. Athletic heroes are timeless. There is nothing in this classic photo of Ali's triumph over Sonny Liston that the Greek poet Pindar would not have recognized.

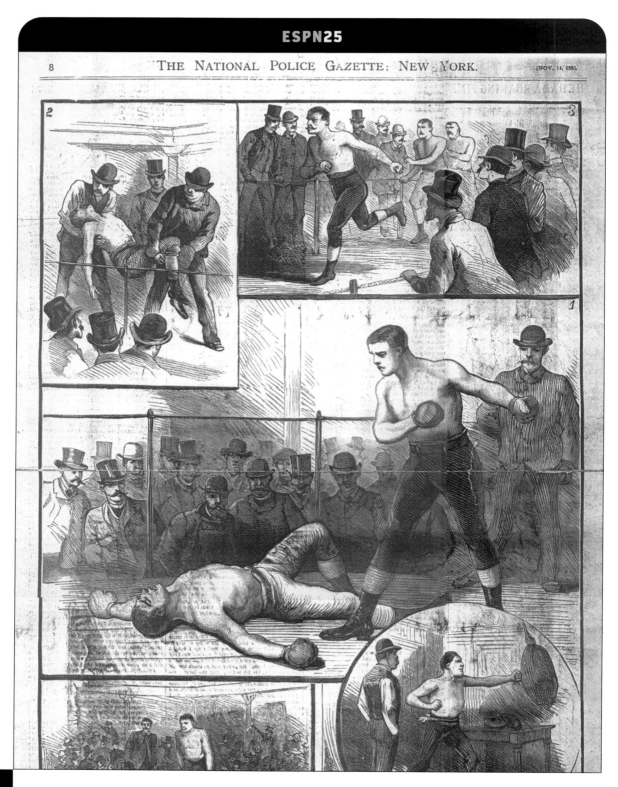

away on their shoulders. Not a single moment of the game itself was ever mentioned.

Even when the on-field action was acknowledged, many writers of the 1870s seemed clueless about how to describe it. A *New York Times* report of the 1878 Harvard-Yale baseball game artfully described the crowd of 5,000: "[The] Harvard men who occupied one end of the Grand Stand were gorgeous with crimson and waved the great crimson flag that floated yesterday before the Harvard quarters on the Thames, and the silken trophies won by the Harvard [rowing team] on that river." As for the baseball game, "the playing was never better"; but you'd never know it from the account that followed: "Harvard made in the first inning 1 run, in the second 4 runs, in the third none . . . . " And it went on: "Yale made nothing in the first four innings, 2 in the fifth, nothing in the sixth. . . . " The writer was apparently unaware that all of this information was contained in an accompanying box score—invented just a few years earlier by the *New York Herald*'s Henry Chadwick, who was, according to Oriard, the first full-time sports reporter every hired by a daily paper.

But even such lame articles as these helped stoke the national mania for sport, increasing the aroma of excitement and mystique that surrounded it. (How many male readers, for instance, could have overlooked that bit about a huge audience of ladies taking "an equal interest"?) So as the popularity of sports kept ballooning, it became increasingly obvious to newspaper editors that they needed to do a better job of reporting it. And though the idea of paying some clown to do nothing but watch sports surely stuck in the craw of many an editor (for nothing sticks in an editor's craw like spending money), sportswriters were as inevitable as death and taxes. They came along in the 1880s and '90s, just as all hell was breaking loose in U.S. newspapers, courtesy of a scourge of brilliant, creative and not terribly conscientious media entrepreneurs. Joseph Pulitzer bought a sleepy New York daily called the *World* and turned it into what scholars now consider the "first modern newspaper." For Pulitzer, and, a little later, William Randolph Hearst, sports was a perfect subject for tabloid-style exploitation. Unlike most news events, you always knew ahead of time exactly when a big game was going to happen, so you could hype it in advance and get your reporters to the scene on time, even if they were drunk. When it was over, a newspaper behaved very much like a Greek god,

"I don't know if **my behavior** has **improved** much with age. They just found someone **worse.**"

—Jimmy Connors

Read all about it
The National Police Gazette, *an extremely popular and shamelessly lurid tabloid, covered sports, and especially boxing, much the way media does today—with vivid highlights. An 1885 issue (opposite) shows "all-conquering Jack Dempsey [knocking out] Dave Campbell after a sharp encounter in Portland, Ore."*

"There's a **soft liner** which is caught by the second baseman. And the ball **game is over— for this inning.**"

—Jerry Coleman, Padres broadcaster

bestowing kudos on the heroes and heaping scorn on the goats.

Oriard has told the tale of this revolution in a book called *Reading Football*. In 1880, for instance, three years before Pulitzer arrived, *The World* surrendered just two unillustrated columns to the nation's biggest football game, Princeton vs. Yale. A few years after Pulitzer took over, half the front page was devoted to that game, under a headline that screamed, TIGERS ALL! (meaning that Princeton had won). There were drawings of pileups and scrambles, and a diagram that traced the path of the ball up and down the gridiron as if it were some mysterious scientific phenomenon. A few years down the line, coverage of big games would go on for pages, with one set aside for "Snapshots of Actual Plays on the Football Field." They were, in fact, drawings (photography was still rare in newspapers) and the "actual plays" were selected by the artist pretty much at random: "Capt. Hinkey of Yale dropping on the ball," or "Capt. Emmons of Harvard about to tackle." They weren't highlights by today's standards, since no attempt was made to isolate key moments of the contest. But such sketches were a major, if toddling, step in the general direction of *SportsCenter*. And occasional stories came a good deal nearer than that.

A *Harper's Weekly* article from August 1885 reported, with some surprise, that anyone, no matter how pompous, could have a grand time at a baseball game. "The people [of New York] manifest less interest in a Presidential election than in a baseball contest in which the New Yorks and Chicagoes cross bats," observed the amazed author, who decided to see for himself what all the fuss was about. He made his way to the Polo Grounds, where an astonishing 7,043 fans were in attendance. By the 10th inning, the game was still scoreless and the writer, almost beside himself with excitement, recorded the climactic highlight with as much enthusiasm as his dignity would allow. Both the scene, and the emotions that underlie it, are wonderfully familiar to a 21st-century sports fan, despite the author's flatulent 19th-century bombast.

"EWING, the catcher of the New Yorks," he wrote, "moved

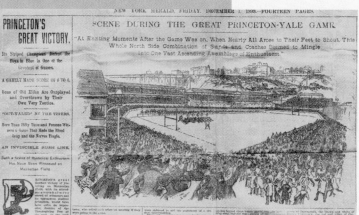

"Give them plenty of pictures"
Nineteenth-century newspapers often focused more attention on stadium crowds than on actual games, as in this front-page illustration from an 1893 New York Herald.

the stick nervously up and down as the Chicago pitcher, cool, imperturbable, and with unerring aim, sent in a hot shot. There was a flash, as of a flail in the hands of a thresher, and out into the right field went the surprised ball." The poor ball was surprised again when a hit-and-run advanced EWING to third, and yet again, when "GILLESPIE, tall and lanky" hit a chopper to second. EWING broke from third, "his legs twinkled as he ran, and his head was bent forward on his breast. . . . Like a bullet from a gun the ball left the right hand of the Chicagoes' second base man and came whizzing in toward the plate . . . EWING made a dive. A cloud of dust arose from the home plate, and when it cleared away, EWING was seen lying on the ground, his finger-tips touching the plate. The ball lay on the ground just behind him, and Catcher Flint, half blinded by the dust, was looking aimlessly for it."

Such narratives were crucial to the growth of American sports—even more crucial, Oriard believes, than the television coverage of the 1960s that would make football the U.S.'s most popular sport. It was the improbable combination of hype (TIGERS ALL!) and educational highlights ("Actual Plays") that transformed football "from an extracurricular activity into a national spectacle."

O ther sports benefited from the new media almost as much. Richard Kyle Fox cannot be held responsible for the Fox network of today, but he was definitely its spiritual godfather. His in-your-face tabloid, *The National Police Gazette*, was printed on eye-catching pink paper (an odd choice for a males-only sheet). Though it boasted a hefty circulation of 150,000, it was far more widely read than that, as there was scarcely a tavern or barbershop where a well-thumbed copy couldn't be found. Fox's motto: "If they can't read, give them plenty of pictures," and since many of them couldn't, the *Gazette* was loaded with vividly drawn highlights.

Fox's passion was boxing, and he didn't just report on it, he was the era's top fight promoter, too, often putting up the prizes himself—more than $250,000 worth over the course of his career. (According to Rader, Fox also sponsored contests for teeth lifting, female weightlifting and one-legged clog dancing.) No one was more responsible for creating the country's first national sports celebrity: heavyweight champion John L. Sullivan.

The *Gazette* all but made Sullivan, who amassed (and

"He made a **stupid call** and it will be **stupid** till the day he dies. **He's Stupid Hank.** That's his nickname. It was a bogus call and he did a **stupid thing.** But we're all human."
—Charles Barkley, after being ejected by a referee named Hank

■ For the past 25 years, they've been the best places to watch and the best places to play (or, for opponents, the worst). They've provided those at the ballparks and arenas plenty to cheer about, and great players and teams to cheer for. They're the top 17 venues of the past quarter century.

1. Wrigley Field Even without a World Series, it's given us great times. Sammy Sosa and the '98 home run race. Pete Rose tying Ty Cobb's hit mark. Harry Caray leading the fans in "Take Me Out to the Ballgame."

2. Cameron Indoor Stadium One of the biggest indoor arenas when it opened in 1940, it's now one of the smallest. No matter. With 9,314 "Cameron Crazies" packed into Duke's cozy hoops venue, opponents don't stand much of a chance.

3. Lambeau Field The Packers' stadium in frigid Green Bay is imbued with the spirit of Vince Lombardi, and filled with the fannies of thousands of team owners/fans.

4. Chicago Stadium / United Center Take some of the most intimidating fans in sports. Add six NBA titles, Michael Jordan, Zen master Phil Jackson roaming the sidelines and a dash of Ray Clay on the mike. It doesn't get much better.

5. SBC Park (formerly Pac Bell Park) Barry Bonds: the record-breaking homers No. 71-73 in 2001. Then there was the great World Series against the Angels in 2002—remember the home plate rescue of Dusty Baker's son?

6. Joe Louis Arena Opened in 1979, and home to three Stanley Cup–winning Red Wings teams. These and other playoff wins called for lots of octopi on ice, one of the strangest of U.S. fan traditions ever.

7. Notre Dame Stadium Blessed by Touchdown Jesus and familiar to every *Rudy* fan, the stadium seats 80,000 and has probably been seen on TV more than any other college football stadium, thanks to ND's national following.

8. Fenway Park It hasn't changed much since opening in 1912, but old Fenway has given us some treasures of late: Roger Clemens striking out 20; the 1986 World Series; and the heart-stopping 2003 playoffs against the A's and Yanks.

9. Yankee Stadium How many October moments and World Series wins can we recount? The horseshoe-shaped stadium has it all—great teams, the Boss, bleacher creatures, celebs, Monument Park . . . and now, even A-Rod.

10. Boston Garden Opened in 1928, the Garden was definitely showing its age when the great frontline of Bird, McHale and Parish pounded the arena's parquet floor. But who cares? Not Boston fans who saw sixteen NBA titles won there.

11. Conseco Fieldhouse Where better to see pro hoops than Indiana? Conseco is the first "retro" arena, and has seen some fantastic finishes since its first pro game in 1999—courtesy of clutch sharpshooter Reggie Miller.

12. The Forum/Staples Center The Showtime Lakers of Magic, Kareem, James Worthy and Pat Riley. The current version with Shaq, Kobe and Phil. Plus an endless roster of revolving movie stars, led by Jack Nicholson.

13. Daytona International Speedway About 200,000 fans cram in to see the Daytona 500 every February, and they've seen it all, from Dale Earnhardt's long-awaited first win in 1998 to the tragic crash that took No. 3's life in 2001.

14. Mile High Stadium 320 games. 250 straight sellouts. Four AFC title games. The loudest fans, the altitude, the cold weather that made Mile High one of the toughest road games in the NFL. And who will ever forget "The Fumble"?

15. Michie Stadium At 80, it's one of the oldest college football stadiums, and maybe the best. It's perched right on the Hudson, and the thousands of screaming cadets and alums provide an intense game-day atmosphere.

16. Oriole Park at Camden Yards The first "retro" ballpark opened in 1992, and some say it's still the best. Its greatest moment: Iron Man Cal Ripken, Jr. breaking the unbreakable, and O's fans standing for 22 minutes in salute.

17. Arrowhead Stadium The Chiefs have one of the best home-field advantages in the NFL. And there's been plenty of excitement in KC, including six straight playoff appearances beginning in 1990.

BEST DRAFT PICKS

■ There are varying levels of sophistication in all forms of drafting, but bottom line: In all sports, drafts have become far more complicated over the past 25 years. Potential NFL draftees undergo unbelievable scrutiny, and have for years. Foreign players have become the new wild card in the NBA—where's the next Dirk Nowitzki coming from? The result: The NFL and NBA drafts, especially, have become huge events in and of themselves.

1. Dan Marino, Dolphins

Twenty-six teams passed on Marino before the Dolphins selected him in the 1983 draft. Among the QBs picked before Marino: Todd Blackledge, Tony Eason and Ken O'Brien.

2. Michael Jordan, Bulls
Selected third in the 1984 NBA draft.

3. Mike Piazza, Dodgers

The future Hall of Famer, the greatest hitting catcher of all time, was selected by the Dodgers in the 62nd round of the 1988 draft.

4. Jerry Rice, 49ers
Fifteen players went before Rice, from Mississippi Valley State, in the 1985 draft, but the 49ers knew what he could do. "The knock was he wasn't fast enough," said Bill Walsh. "All I ever saw on film was him running away from players."

5. John Stockton, Jazz
Picked 16th in the 1984 draft.

6. Brett Favre, Falcons

The great Packers QB, a HOF shoe-in, wasn't picked until the second round of the 1991 draft.

7. Emmitt Smith, Cowboys
Sixteen picks went by in the 1990 draft before the Cowboys selected the man who would become the NFL's all-time leading rusher.

8. Terrell Davis, Broncos
One hundred and ninety-five players were selected before the Broncos nabbed Davis in the 1995 draft. What they got was one of the greatest running backs of all time, a key to victories in Super Bowls XXXII and XXXIII.

9. Kobe Bryant, Lakers
Twelve teams passed before the Hornets picked him in 1996—and traded him to the Lakers for Vlade Divac.

10. Karl Malone, Jazz
Thirteenth pick in the 1985 draft.

11. John Smoltz, Tigers
Most teams passed on him in the 1985 draft, thinking Smoltzie college bound. The Tigers took a 22nd-round chance, though, and it was a small, but very smart, gamble. It paid off two years later, when the Tigers traded Smoltz to the Braves and picked up Doyle Alexander. Alexander went 9-0 in the stretch run, propelling the Tigers to the AL East title by two games over Toronto.

12. Andy Pettitte, Yankees
Picked in the 22nd round in 1990.

13. Jose Canseco, A's
Picked up by Oakland in the 15th round of the 1982 draft.

14. Brett Hull, Calgary Flames
Selected 117th in the 1984 NHL draft.

15. Richard Dent, Bears
Dent, a four-time Pro Bowler as a defensive end, was the 203rd pick in the 1983 draft. In his 15 NFL seasons, he recorded 137.5 sacks. Dent was also the Super Bowl XX MVP.

16. Jeff Bagwell, Red Sox

Bagwell was a third baseman for the University of Hartford when the Red Sox selected him in the fourth round of the 1989 draft. Two years later, he was the NL Rookie of the Year, and was the NL MVP in 1994. The same Sox who were smart enough to draft him unfortunately lacked the foresight to keep him.

17. Jim Thome, Indians
Picked in the 13th round in 1989 out of Illinois Central Junior College.

18. Jorge Posada, Yankees
Selected in the 24th round in 1990.

19. Karl Mecklenburg, Broncos

Mecklenburg, a defensive lineman, went to six Pro Bowls in his 12-year career, which began in 1983, after the Broncos selected him with the 310th pick in that year's draft.

20. Reggie Lewis, Celtics
Twenty-second pick overall in the 1987 draft.

21. Latrell Sprewell, Golden State
Picked 24th in the 1992 draft.

22. Lenny Dykstra, Mets
Picked in the 12th round of the 1981 draft.

23. Vlade Divac, L.A. Lakers
Selected 26th in the 1989 NBA draft.

24. Patrick Roy, Montreal Canadiens
Fifty players were selected before the Canadiens picked the future Hall of Fame goalie in the third round of the 1984 NHL entry draft.

25. Zach Thomas, Miami Dolphins
A fifth-round pick in 1996.

drank up) a fortune giving exhibitions throughout the country. Many of his bouts were arranged in the paper's offices and promoted in its pages for months. Sullivan would be shown in a top hat, giving money to a distressed, but grateful, widow; the taunts of his opponents would be relayed to him, and vice versa, by the *Gazette*'s busy reporters; and the final result would be delivered to readers with as much lurid violence as possible. Fox showed the nation how to profit from spectator sports: Create the stars, get them under contract and make the real money not so much from the event itself as from the media coverage of it.

But the burgeoning sports market would soon outgrow him, for he was just too crude. In 1892, when Sullivan finally fought the bout of his life against Gentleman Jim Corbett, the fight was arranged not by Fox, but by Pulitzer. And, in a nod to civilization that disgusted *Gazette* readers, the fighters wore gloves. Beyond this, even as Corbett was taking Sullivan's title in a lopsided 21-round New Orleans brawl, a new technology was emerging—one that would alter people's perception of life in general, and sports in particular, forevermore. ∎

"There'll be **two buses** leaving the hotel for the park tomorrow. The **two o'clock bus** will be for those of you **who need a little extra work.** The **empty bus** will be leaving at **five o'clock.**"
—S.F. Giants manager Dave Bristol, to his team

Play of the day
White Stockings vs. Giants, 1885

CHAPTER 2

The Flickering Fistic Peep Show

THOMAS EDISON ERECTED AMERICA'S FIRST FILM STUDIO IN West Orange, New Jersey, in 1892, at a cost of $637.67. He christened it the Kinetographic Theater, but everyone else called it the "Black Maria." At first glance, it looked like a barn wrapped in tar paper. But its roof was designed to swing open, much like the back end of a paddy wagon (for which "black maria" was slang in those days). The Maria was also set a few feet off the ground on a mechanical pivot so that the whole building could be swung around to follow the arc of the sun. All of this was to provide a steady stream of natural light for Edison's newest gadget, the Kinetograph.

This early motion-picture camera produced 30-second flicks for an arcade contraption called the Kinetoscope, or "Peep Show." The camera was as big as a doghouse and couldn't be moved, so anything Edison or his business partners wanted to film had to be brought to the Black Maria. They began importing vaudeville acts they figured men would cheerfully part with a nickel to see: A strongman named "Sandow, the Modern Hercules" flexed his abdominals; Carmencita, a dancer from Koster & Bial's Music Hall, twirled her skirt naughtily. But the inventors soon tired of that sort of thing and itched to film something live, unpredictable and dramatic. The problem was, something had to take place inside the Black Maria. In July of 1894, a perfect solution was discovered: boxing.

The "Black Maria" Edison's New Jersey studio, with its openable roof, where sports and motion pictures coupled for the first time in 1894.

> "To me, **boxing** is **like a ballet,** except there's **no music,** no **choreography** and the **dancers hit each other.**"
>
> —Jack Handey, "Deep Thoughts," *Saturday Night Live*

Two lightweights, Michael Leonard and Jack Cushing, entered the tiny studio and fought an uncomfortable 6-round bout in front of the Kinetograph. The fight, won by Leonard, was then presented to the public in six separate peep-show machines (one for each round), set side by side. According to Raymond Fielding, Dean Emeritus of Florida State's film school, the Leonard-Cushing fight ranks as the first film of a news event (broadly defined, but he's the dean) ever made in the U.S. It also established sports' central place in the filmed news industry—a wacky genre of movie-house infotainment that nonetheless laid the groundwork for the sports highlight of today.

The newborn movie business became addicted to boxing, for what was better suited to a small rectangular screen than a sport that took place in a small rectangular ring? A few months after Leonard vs. Cushing, heavyweight champion Gentleman Jim Corbett arrived at the Black Maria to knock out an obscure

The first live, filmed sporting event, in fact, the first live, filmed news event of any kind featured Leonard and Cushing in a makeshift ring inside Edison's Black Maria.

challenger named Peter Courtney. This was a more dramatic fight and it made a far more popular peep show. It was also a sham: Corbett was paid a reported $4,750 to make the "fight" look interesting for five reels, and then pretend to flatten Courtney just before the Kinetograph ran out of film. According to Fielding, this event gave boxing "the dubious distinction of being the [subject of the] first *fake* news film ever produced."

One question remained: Were audiences paying to see sports, or were they paying to see the novelty of motion pictures? The issue was settled in 1897 after a savage 14-round match between Corbett and Bob Fitzsimmons that ended with Fitzsimmons's utterly sick blow to Corbett's belly. The Veriscope Company's film of the rumble earned a reputed $750,000.

Competition to film major prizefights grew as fierce as anything inside the ring. In 1899, the Biograph Company set up its equipment inside the Coney Island Athletic Club in order to film a bout between Jim Jeffries and Tom Sharkey. A rival company's crew snuck in with the crowd. They tried to look nonchalant, but their cameraman had a huge camera stuffed under his overcoat and, according to a companion, he resembled "someone astride a small horse." Biograph had hired thugs from the Pinkerton Detective Agency to guard their exclusive and the interlopers were soon spotted. But Jeffries vs. Sharkey turned out to be such a barn burner, the Pinkertons couldn't get through the delirious crowd to stop them. On it went for 25 vicious rounds, under 300 white-hot film lights (cornermen shaded the boxers' heads with umbrellas as they sat on their stools), both cameras whirring. Jeffries finally pulled it out, then dragged himself into the streets of New York along with the Pinkertons in an unsuccessful hunt for the pirate film.

Popular as they were, prizefight movies were doomed by their own success. For centuries, boxing had been off-limits to

"That's great. We'll take 29 players and let the muggers make our final cuts."
—Mets manager Bobby Valentine after learning that his team would play two exhibition games in New Orleans

Da' fight film was all the rage by 1907. Here, in the first round of a heavyweight title bout, Tommy Burns stretches Bill Squires, takes a long, contemptuous look at his victim, and then rides away.

everyone but saloon-going males. Without warning, film had set the sport before the entire public. It is impossible to imagine the horror such movies inflicted on prim folks, unused to either violence or cinema. Here was a black-and-white nightmare of giant, ghostly men, stripped to the waist (which in itself was indecent to many moviegoers of the time), socking one another to the rhythm of organ music while fight fans whooped for blood.

The last straw came in 1910, when African-American Jack Johnson knocked the daylights out of white Jim Jeffries to become the world's first black heavyweight champion—a subversive spectacle made much "worse" by endless repetition in movie houses throughout the land. Even Theodore Roosevelt, America's favorite man's man, denounced boxing movies and called for their suppression. Sure enough, in 1912, the Sims Act made it illegal to transport boxing films from one state to another, effectively putting them to an end for a generation.

FAIREST ZEBRAS

■ The toughest list in this book to compile. We have a pretty good idea who the really "bad" refs and umps are these days, because the blown calls are replayed ad infinitum on the highlight reels.

But the best? We scouted out as much public domain info as we could find—player and coach polls, the occasional leak of league evaluations—and narrowed it down to the fairest of the best.

1. Earl Strom (NBA)

No. 1 NBA referee among players when he retired in 1989-90, favored by, among others, Bill Russell, Julius Erving and Michael Jordan. The only Hall of Famer from the last 25 years, Strom was an NBA ref for 32 years, and he had both style and guts. While teams playing away won only 30 percent of the time with other refs calling the game, they won 40 percent when Strom was on the court—he was unafraid of hometown fans. "He always had control of the game," said former Cavaliers general manager Wayne Embry. "If he thought things were getting out of hand, he'd go up to this guy, go up to that guy and let them know he was running the game. What I liked about him as much as anything is that when he blew a call, he admitted he blew a call. He acknowledged it. There are not many around today who will do that."

2. Andy Van Hellemond (NHL)

Van Hellemond worked his first NHL game in 1972, and his last in 1996. For 14 consecutive years, he was the NHL's top-rated referee, and set a slew of records: most regular season games refereed—1,475; most playoff games—227; and most appearances as a ref in the Stanley Cup Finals—19. In 1999, he was inducted into the Hockey Hall of Fame.

3. Jerry Markbreit (NFL)

Markbreit retired after the 1998 season, his 23rd as an NFL ref. The league chooses its best for the Super Bowl, and Markbreit was clearly a top arbiter, having

been chosen to ref four Super Bowls—XVII, XXI, XXVI and XXIX. "He was the epitome of what officiating in the NFL is all about," said senior director of officiating Jerry Seeman when Markbreit hung up his whistle.

4. Jake O'Donnell (NBA)

In 1992, SI polled NBA coaches and general managers, and three fourths of them said O'Donnell (who retired after 28 years in December, 1995) was the best—by far—not just ready but very able to be top dog after the retirement of Earl Strom. "He's the game's ombudsman," said one coach. Incredibly, from 1968 to 1971, before he ever set foot on NBA hardwood, O'Donnell was one of MLB's best umpires. In 1970, he was selected to the elite crew that umpired the American League Championship Series.

5. Steve Palermo (MLB)

Palermo was only 26 years old when he first umped a Major League game. Sixteen years later, in 1991, many considered him the best in baseball. Then, one night after a game, he chased down muggers outside a restaurant in Dallas, and was rewarded for his effort by being shot—and hit—by a man in the getaway car. That ended his career on the field; Palermo is now MLB's supervisor of umpires. Sympathy call? No way. On-field reputation? Way. He was very, very good. He's "in a class of his own," said one AL catcher in 1987. "He hustles, and he's consistent. I just enjoy working with him."

So filmmakers turned, with even greater energy, to other sports. Just as the Sims Act became law, the newsreel—that 10-minute potpourri of news, human interest and sports that would shape public attitudes immeasurably in the first half of the 20th century—began to appear in theaters. Pathé, Fox, Hearst and many other companies began battling over sports stories like so many Crips and Bloods. The stakes were high, since sports would account for 20 percent of newsreel content in the 1920s (and would rise to 25 percent by the late 1930s).

This competition delighted sports promoters, who began selling exclusive film rights to the highest bidder. That drove the newsreel boys (they were virtually all boys) batty. Many of them were former newspaper reporters and, as such, had always covered sports for free. Why should there be one rule for paper and another for celluloid? They'd storm at the promoters, swearing they'd never pay, but ultimately one newsreel company or another would break down and cough up a substantial sum— knowing full well that most of their competitors would try to film pirate versions of the event. Any game of consequence was infested with unauthorized cameramen, crouching in their seats or pretending to sell sarsaparilla in the aisles or hovering in a nearby water tower while security guards pursued them like Keystone Kops.

This gangland rivalry turned to all-out war in 1923 when August Belmont, owner of the Belmont Park raceway, approached Fox's Truman Talley with a remarkable offer. The Pathé company, Belmont told him, was ready to pay $50,000 for rights to film the long-awaited race between champions Zev and Papyrus. Was Talley willing to up the ante?

Talley was so enraged by this shakedown that he decided to spare no expense in making Pathé's exclusive worthless. He arranged a strategic truce with his rivals at Hearst and, between them, the two companies sent more than 40 shooters to Belmont. In his book *The American Newsreel*, Fielding

"Mike Tyson's **not** all that **bad**. If you dig deep . . . dig real deep. **Dig, dig, dig, dig, dig**. Deep, deep. Go all the way to China . . . I'm sure you'll find there's a **nice guy** in there."
—George Foreman

"The Fight of the Century," between white Jim Jeffries and African-American Jack Johnson, had all the trappings of a modern media event. But Johnson's taunting victory appalled so many white Americans that fight films would be outlawed for decades.

"The key to this whole business is sincerity. Once you can fake that, you've got it made."

—Former Lions coach Monte Clark on relating to today's players

records that cameras were staked out in an ice factory across from the track, in specially built camouflaged platforms in nearby trees and in two airplanes leased for the occasion. More than 20 more shooters snuck in as paying customers with cameras under their clothing; eight more were hidden in a horse trailer and trucked onto the grounds; and one actually managed to get hired as a deputized thug, charged with guarding the raceway from illicit cameramen like himself. Besieged, Pathé counterattacked by planting dozens of smoke bombs around the track that were set off the moment the horses left the gate. The idea was to obstruct the interlopers' cameras, but predictably it obstructed their own just as much. Pathé also pointed mirrors toward the ice factory, hoping the reflected light would spoil any film shot from within. But they were hopelessly outgunned; not only did Fox and Hearst get plenty of film, they actually got it into their newsreels a week ahead of Pathé. According to Fielding, "Talley's successful campaign virtually brought an end (until the advent of television) to the practice of purchasing or assigning newsreel rights to sports events." The modern age of sports media was set to begin.

Like three intergalactic villains (or superheroes, depending on your point of view), newsreels, radio and the daily papers joined forces to provide new ways to experience sports. Every paper of consequence now had a sports section, very much like the ones we know today. (According to Oriard, "sports coverage increased by 50 percent over the first two decades of the 20th century, then more than doubled in the 1920s.")

But two distinct "schools" of sportswriting emerged, and, with them, two very different ways of reporting highlights.

The first, The Sunday School, considered athletic competition a sacred experience, a rite of passage where young men acquired the strength of character that made this country great.

This approach left little room for yuks. Grantland Rice, the bard of The Sunday School, is best remembered for describing Notre Dame's 1924 backfield thus: "Outlined against a blue-gray sky, the Four Horsemen rode again. In dramatic lore they were known as Famine, Pestilence, Destruction and Death. These are only aliases. Their real names are Stuhldreher, Miller, Crowley and Layden."

The Sunday School was opposed by The School of Wiseacres. These writers considered sports not as training for

life, but a *part* of life. And life, as they saw it, was full of ironies. Ring Lardner, one of the original Wiseacres, used to love to write as if he was both illiterate and drunk. (Indeed, Lardner often slurped enough booze to make the act completely realistic.) To a Sunday Schooler like Rice, a World Series had all the sanctity of a ritual; but a Wiseacre like Lardner would gleefully poke fun at, say, how absurd it was, in the pre-lights era, to play baseball at twilight. "I would try to describe the game to you in intimate detail was it not played in such darkness that I was only able to see a few incidence [sic]," he wrote of a Giants–Yankees clash in the 1920s. "[One] of these few occurred in the 3rd innings and consisted of [Yankees outfielder] Whitey Witt getting caught asleep off of first base by a snap throw. . . . The dean of Cleveland baseball experts explained this incidence by saying that Whitey thought he was still with the Athletics. It is more likely, however, that Whitey was deceived by the darkness and thought it was his bedtime."

The culture war between the bards and the wiseacres continues to the present day. There can be little doubt which school presently holds sway at ESPN. Let's just say that Grantland Rice would never, ever have called a pitcher Frank Tanana Daiquiri, but Ring Lardner might have. However, in the 1920s and '30s, the Sunday Schoolers ruled with a scowl, especially on the radio, where women and kids were a huge part of the audience.

Radio's first great sportscaster was Graham McNamee, a fast-talking, excitable fellow widely criticized for his ignorance of sports. He got away with it because most fans in those days knew even less than he did, and besides, it was the drama of sports that kept them glued to the speakers, not its subtleties. Consequently, highlights, which are generally too short to provide much drama, were not very radio-friendly.

Not that radio didn't try. Legendary sportscaster Warner Wolf fondly remembers a CBS radio program from his boyhood in which sportscasters would phone in college football results, and occasional highlights, one after another as the games

The drama king *Sports highlights were rarely popular on radio, except when the emotional Bill Stern (above, left) recited them on* The Colgate Sports Newsreel— *often invigorating them with imaginative details he made up as he went along.*

wound down. In 1966, Wolf tried to resuscitate the genre at Washington's WTOP radio, launching an NFL program called *Two Minutes to Go*. He hired stringers in eight or so cities and each one would call up late in the fourth quarter with a report. "They might run down the highlights. But if a game had an exciting finish, we'd get a live running commentary," he recalls. "It could be quite a show." But there were problems, too. Once, Wolf's Philadelphia stringer, Red McCarthy, was excitedly describing a close finish between the Cowboys and Eagles. The 'Boys trailed, 17-16, but quarterback Don Meredith had his offense on the march, deep in Philly territory. "Meredith drops back to pass," McCarthy barked with excitement, "He throws, and . . . aaagh! Aaagh. Aaaaaaaaaagh!"

Wolf still gets a chuckle out of it after four decades. "Red was screaming and the crowd was screaming, and you could hear him pounding on the table. The Cowboys had fumbled, or something, but he was so excited he couldn't speak. He just went on like that—'Aaagh! Aaagh!'—for, I don't know, it seemed like an *eternity*."

By far the most successful highlight show on radio was *The Colgate Sports Newsreel*, and it is hard to imagine an offering more different from *SportsCenter*, both in purpose and tone. In a voice that practically choked with manly emotion, announcer Bill Stern would recount implausibly dramatic moments in sports history. "He told tales of horse races won by dead jockeys, of limbless baseball players, of any thread-thin influences sport had had on the lives of the great," writes radio historian John Dunning. "Occasionally, he told the same story twice (allowing for a decent time span between the tellings), using conflicting facts and passing both versions off as true."

Radio was far better suited to reporting live sports, and its influence on modern highlights lies mostly in the descriptive styles pioneered by its legendary announcers. Baseball was king of the dial. The long, calm stretches where nothing much happened were like a slow vise, tightening until something incredible occurred and the announcer yelled himself hoarse. The newsreels were just the opposite. "They are the true ancestors of *SportsCenter*," says Oriard. "Every game was a big game, every play was a great play, every crowd cheered wildly."

The basic formula was well established by the 1930s: You began with a shot of the crowd (cheering wildly), then showed a climactic play or two and closed with a tight shot of the tri-

"The father of us all" *That's what sportscaster Dick Enberg would later call radio's Graham McNamee* (above), *the voice of American sports in the '20s and '30s.*

umphant hero. The narrator would read a pun-filled script ("*Red Grange* is king of the *green*!") and, sometimes, a dull-eyed player would read from a prepared script ("I'll say me and the fellas are ready for the Cardinals. And how!"). There was no expert commentary, and very little slow motion; not only was it costly, owners hated it for exposing the mistakes of officials. Nor was the footage likely to show the best moments of a game, as cameramen were pressed for both money and time. It wasn't unusual for them to shoot a little film of each side scoring and then use the best film they had of the winning team. As a result, newsreel highlights are incredibly uneven. "Sometimes they'd get lucky," says Oriard. "When Red Grange ran and threw for six touchdowns against Michigan in 1924, four were in the first quarter, so they got all four of 'em."

Baseball, on the other hand, presented immense challenges to the newsreels. Cameras showed up at the World Series for the first time in 1908, when Frank Chance's Cubs beat Hughie Jennings's Tigers (it's a good thing they got it on film, as the Cubs have not won since). But the field was so big, and the ball so small, it was difficult to show one without losing sight of the other. Worse, baseball action often takes place in two or more places at once: Suppose Joe Tinker was sprinting homeward while Chance was barreling toward third. Where were you supposed to point the camera?

Despite vast improvements in newsreel technology over the next half century, the problem was never really solved. In fact, it was made worse, as anxious owners feared good newsreel footage might cut into attendance at the ballpark and began a long history of restricting camera access. "I've seen tons of baseball newsreels," says baseball historian Daniel Okrent, "and almost all of them are bad. Even Enos Slaughter's mad dash home in the '46 World Series is terribly unthrilling, because the cameramen were shooting from such terrible positions. All you really see is Slaughter rounding the bases and the ball coming in late."

No event in modern memory demonstrated the power of sports, for both good and ill, as much as the 1936 Olympic Games, hosted in Berlin by Adolf Hitler. More than 40 percent of Americans had favored a U.S. boycott of the event, a fact that American Olympic Committee chairman Avery Brundage attributed to "contemptible tactics" by "Jews and Communists." On the other hand, many Americans had

"I think we **probably expose our players** to the **media** as well as anybody."
—Michigan State football coach George Perles on female sportswriters in the locker room

> ## "Statistics are used like a drunk uses a lamp post—for support, not illumination."
> —Vin Scully

The triumph of Leni Riefenstahl (above, with a camera crew) *was called* Olympia, *a three-and-a-half-hour collection of highlights from the 1936 Olympic Games in Nazi Germany. Pioneering a host of original techniques, Riefenstahl produced spectacular images of sport never before seen, such as the one at right, from a diving event.*

favored participation because they hoped American victories would belie Nazi boasts of racial superiority. As it turned out, everyone saw what they wanted to see: To Nazis, the Master Race was vindicated by Germany's first place in the medal standings; to American liberals, racism was mocked by the dramatic track-and-field victories of Jesse Owens.

But shortly after the games ended came irrefutable proof of the folly of racism: highlights. Nazi filmmaker Leni Riefenstahl had been given carte blanche to record the games for the silver screen. The result, a three-and-a-half-hour film called *Olympia*, remains the most spectacular collection of sports highlights ever filmed, a document sure to silence anyone who questions the aesthetic value of spectator sports. No idea was too outlandish for Riefenstahl to try, if it might produce an unprecedented shot. She dug a trench beneath the pole vault and photographed the athletes sailing overhead in slow motion, like swooping angels. She rigged up a special wagon that allowed her to whiz alongside the sprinters from the moment they left the blocks. She even tried to rig up a system whereby she could be catapulted in the air in order to film the leaping events, but never figured out how to do it without killing herself. In all, she shot more than 1,300,000 feet of film that took two years to splice together. The result—despite a few minutes of propaganda aimed at glorifying Aryan athletes—glorified all athletes, regardless of race.

The influence of Riefenstahl's masterpiece is difficult to measure. Her artistic approaches were much too costly for the newsreels, especially slow-motion shots, which required a tremendous amount of film. It would be another three decades before slo-mo would become a routine part of American sports highlights. But the 1936 Olympics marked another key breakthrough: The Germans accomplished the world's first sports television broadcast, transmitting to a few dozen *Fernsehstuben* ("television sites") throughout Berlin, where the fluttering miracle was witnessed by an estimated 150,000 viewers.

In the U.S., a long-forgotten Philadelphia football game became the first televised sporting event, sometime in 1938. But the era of televised sports began in earnest the following year, when W2XBS, an NBC station in New York, broadcast a Columbia vs. Princeton baseball game to about 200 sets. A single camera peered at the action as best it could from an uncomfortable position down the third base line. All the prob-

"That picture was taken out of context."
—Mets pitcher Jeff Innis, commenting on an unflattering newspaper photo

Unsurpassed A poster for Riefenstahl's highlight masterpiece.

lems that had bedeviled newsreel photographers in shooting baseball were compounded on the small screen. Early television was constantly beset by breakups in the signal that resulted in "snow"—white dots resembling dozens of tiny baseballs flashing in rows across the screen. It is hard to imagine a better way to torment a devoted sports fan.

And so early TV pioneers did what their predecessors in film had done: focused on the screen-friendly sport of boxing. In '44, Gillette began sponsoring NBC's *Friday Night Fights* broadcasts from Madison Square Garden (later grandiosely renamed the *Gillette Cavalcade of Sports*), with Willie Pep outdueling Chalkie Wright for the featherweight belt in the debut. When World War II ended and newly built homes began to fill up with sets, the networks went fight mad: CBS counterpunched with *Blue Ribbon Bouts* on Wednesdays and little ABC, the runt of the networks, tried to keep pace with *Tomorrow's Boxing Champions*, featuring unranked up-and-comers. By the early 1950s, with well over 10 million TV sets ensconced in American homes, boxing accounted for an astonishing 30 percent of all prime-time viewing. Football, another sport far better suited to the small screen than baseball, thrived, too. In 1950, New Yorkers could choose from at least eight college games every Saturday. There were no sports highlight shows; who needed 'em? What made television so exciting was that it was *live*.

But that was also the problem, at least for the kingpins of both sports and broadcasting. The televising of sports simultaneously boosted and undermined them. Take boxing: With all those high-profile bouts airing for free, who in their right mind would pay to see a fight? The thousands of fight clubs across America, where aspiring pugilists trained and brawled for small local audiences—the sport's lifeblood—began to drop like so many palookas. By 1957, even the Garden was drawing just 1,200 fight fans on an average Friday—one tenth the number it had packed in less than a decade previous.

Football had welcomed television with open arms, but almost immediately, attendance plummeted. Both the NCAA and Bert Bell, autocratic commissioner of the sputtering NFL, drew up onerous national policies dictating which games could be broadcast. Bell also had them blacked out to local viewers. In many cases, even highlights were blacked out.

Baseball, meanwhile, was in full-blown crisis. Its owners knew they couldn't survive without television, but with atten-

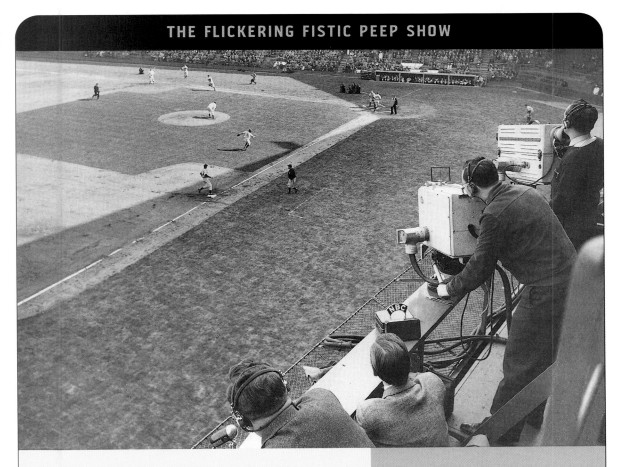

dance already in free fall (due, in large part, to TV), how could they survive with it? Baseball Commissioner Ford Frick's response was to issue a disastrous edict: Though television broadcasts would be permitted, "the view a fan gets at home should not be any better than that of the fan in the worst seat of the ball park." To ensure that TV audiences had a truly lousy view of the proceedings, one camera was allowed to perch somewhere behind the plate while two more sat far away, down the foul lines. On the one hand, Frick's policy encouraged fans to stay home and watch the game on TV; but on the other, it punished them for doing so by making the game appear remote, dull and difficult to follow, especially to the casual fan.

All of which left the barn door open for Bell and his NFL, and they galloped through it like the Four Horsemen, outlined against a blue-gray sky. NBC's broadcast of the 1958 NFL Championship between the Colts and Giants showed just how TV-friendly the gridiron could be. "The Greatest Game Ever Played" transfixed the nation as it went to overtime, climaxed

Great seat, huh? By restricting TV cameras to the worst seats in the house, Commissioner Ford Frick subjected an entire generation of potential fans to baseball at its worst.

43

■ In 1978, fans at the Vet were introduced to the Phillie Phanatic. In June, 1979, came the The Grand Hatching, when Ted Giannoulas, wearing a silly bird suit, cracked open a giant egg before 47,000 Padres fans, and The Famous San Diego Chicken became a star. The Chicken changed everything—he was listed by one magazine as one of the 20th century's most powerful sports people. Mascots are an irreplaceable part of the sports land-scape—and, in recent years, have become a high-lights staple.

■ The Phillie Phanatic

■ The Famous San Diego Chicken *(Padres)*

■ Rocky *(Denver Nuggets)*

■ Ballapeño the Jalapeño and Henry the Puffy Taco *(San Antonio Missions)*

■ Ralphie the Buffalo *(Colorado)*

■ Billy the Marlin *(Florida)*

■ Jaxson DeVille *(Jacksonville Jaguars)*

■ Harvey the Hound *(Calgary Flames)*

■ YoUDee, University of Delaware Fightin' Blue Hen

■ Banana Slug *(University of California, Santa Cruz)*

■ BU's "Rhett," a Boston terrier named after Rhett Butler

■ Mr. Met

■ Edgar, Allan and Poe *(Baltimore Ravens)*

■ Trapper, Chomps, CB and TD *(Cleveland Browns)*

■ Bevo *(University of Texas at Austin)*

■ Bulldog *(Georgia)*

■ Bucky Badger *(University of Wisconsin)*

■ Smokey *(University of Tennessee)*

■ Penn State Nittany Lion

■ Phoenix Suns Gorilla

■ Wool E. Bull *(Durham Bulls)*

■ Aubie the Tiger *(Auburn)*

Improvements & Innovations

■ One of the great things about sports is that, through the years, they remain recognizable—football fields are still 100 yards long, baseball bats (at least in the majors) still made of wood. But every once in a while someone fiddles with the game—or the way the game is presented—and that change is good. We looked for stuff that made things more exciting (the expansion of March Madness), or more fair (instant replay in the NFL), or better for viewers at home (the "1st & Ten" line). And the final criteria? Once these innovations took hold, we didn't want to go back to the way things were.

1. The three-point shot in college and pro basketball

Introduced in 1979-80 in the NBA and in college basketball in '86-'87, the intended effect was to open up the floor. The result was a low-percentage shot that nonetheless gave some teams an extra tool and made a variety of comeback scenarios possible where none existed before.

2. March Madness expansion

In 1978, the NCAA men's basketball tournament included 32 teams in the first round. In 1979, that number grew to 40, in 1980 it expanded again, to 48, and in 1985, the field expanded to 64 teams. In 2001, a play-in round expanded the field to 65 teams. Along the way, the tourney grew into a wildly popular national event in sports. Single elimination, upsets galore, and all kinds of Final Four hope for teams that wouldn't have even been in the tourney before March became Madness.

3. Ever-present time-and-score box and yellow "1st & Ten" line

Fox invented the constant score-and-time display when it began its NFL broadcasts in

continued on page 48

with the Colts' "Thirteen Steps to Glory" drive and ended with fullback Alan Ameche's bull-like TD plunge. Equally heroic was the performance of NBC executive Stan Rotkiewicz. Shortly before the game's denouement, the network's transmission was interrupted by a technical snafu. The quick-thinking Rotkiewicz, pretending to be a drunken fan, lurched onto the field and stopped play long enough for frantic technicians to fix the problem. It was a stroke of sheer genius, for the idea of the Greatest Game Ever Played ending with a test pattern instead of Ameche is too terrible to contemplate. Doubtless Rotkiewicz would be remembered as the Patron Saint of Television Football, if another genius hadn't come along to take that title from him.

Roone Pinckney Arledge entered this adolescent world of sports television in 1960, when he was just 29. His previous TV experience consisted mainly of bossing a New York children's program called *Hi Mom!* featuring ventriloquist Shari Lewis and her lovable sock puppets, Lamb Chop, Hush Puppy and Charlie Horse. Arledge was lured to ABC by a producer named Ed Scherick, who, by a wily bit of backroom chicanery too complicated to explain, had just outfoxed NBC for the rights to broadcast NCAA football. But now that ABC had them, advertisers weren't sure that the notoriously cheap and unimaginative network would know what to do with them. Desperate for new ideas, Scherick hired Arledge for his fresh perspective—and was nearly forced to fire him three days later, when a trade paper revealed that ABC was betting on a "freckle-faced kid . . . who produced a local kiddie show" to produce football games. Scherick stuck by his kid, though, and sports television would never be the same.

Arledge had his first epiphany before the football season even began. Scherick sent him to San Francisco to produce a *Baseball Game of the Week* at Candlestick Park. Arledge looked at the three badly placed stationary cameras, standing like open-mouthed dolts waiting for something to happen, and shook his head. He began to wander through the stands, holding up his fingers in the shape of a screen and looking through them, as Fellini might have done. He marveled to himself that fans at home were missing far more of the spectacle than they were seeing. TV's whole approach to sports was wrong, he declared to Scherick; it was, he said, "like looking out on the Grand Canyon through a peephole in a door." A few Sundays later, Arledge sat down at his home in Armonk, New York, opened a beer, and

typed one of the most seminal manifestos in television history.

"Heretofore, television has done a remarkable job of bringing the game to the viewer," he began, so as not to offend anyone. "Now we are going to take the viewer to the game!" He would use six "fixed" cameras, he explained, but each shooter would be required to "cover all the other interesting facets of the game when he is not actually engaged in covering a game situation." That would be a change, but he was just getting warmed up. "We will have cameras mounted in Jeeps, on mike booms, in risers or helicopters," he went on. "We will use a 'creepie-peepie' [portable] camera to get the impact shots that we cannot get from a fixed camera—a coach's face as a man drops a pass in the clear—a pretty cheerleader after her hero has scored a touchdown—a coed who brings her infant baby to the game—the referee as he calls a particularly difficult play—two romantic students sharing a blanket late in the game on a cold day—the beaming face of a substitute halfback as he comes off the field after running seventy yards for a touchdown. . . . In short—WE ARE GOING TO ADD SHOW BUSINESS TO SPORTS!"

Even allowing for the salesmanship in Arledge's memo, there is no mistaking his genuine excitement. The point of view he proposed would become not only the fundamental landscape for virtually all sports television, but one of the defining tableaus of American culture.

In 1960, though, it was so revolutionary, Arledge had a hell of a time selling it. "I sure hope in the middle of all this stuff you get around to showin' some *football*," growled legendary NFL quarterback Paul Christman, the color man ABC had hired to call the games with play-by-play announcer Curt Gowdy. But the critics fell silent after Arledge's first NCAA broadcast, a Georgia vs. Alabama contest at Legion Field. "However imperfectly," Arledge would later write in his memoir, *Roone* (published just after his death in 2002), "we used the violent meeting of twenty-two young men to do something

Prime-time pigskin *The Colts' heart-stopping overtime victory over the Giants in the 1958 NFL championship game proved to a national audience that football and television were made for each other. No one saw the potential more clearly than Roone Arledge, mastermind of modern sports television, below with his Monday Night Football stars, "Dandy" Don Meredith and Howard Cosell.*

continued from page 46

1994; some viewers complained, calling it distracting, but as you know, it caught on, and is now a permanent fixture in TV broadcasts of almost all sports events.

The "1st & Ten" line, an Emmy Award–winning innovation developed by SportVision and first used by ESPN in September 1998, is an overlay that only TV viewers can see. It portrays the accurate distance to a first down and required, initially, three specially designed TV cameras, eight computers and several technicians.

4. Retro ballparks

Beginning with Oriole Park at Camden Yards, which opened in Baltimore in 1992, baseball caught "retro" fever. Retro parks are designed to combine the best elements of old ballparks—seats close to the action, traditional brick-and-steel architecture, hand-operated scoreboards and the like—with modern amenities.

5. Instant replay in the NFL

Officials make mistakes. Lots, if you listen to the losers. Some, if you listen to the winners (and according to the winners, they all balance out). In 1986, when the instant replay rule was introduced, the NFL came clean: Not only do officials make mistakes, it was admitting that sometimes those mistakes are big and obvious and cost games. And the league also said: We have the technology to do something about it. With instant replay, coaches can now selectively challenge officials' calls, and get a fair hearing. It's simple: Instant replay makes most games more fair.

6. Rotisserie/fantasy sports leagues

The first Rotisserie league was formed in January 1980, by Dan Okrent, Glen Waggoner and others. In the league, owners drafted players from real teams, and their compiled statistics were tallied up at the end of the real season to produce a Rotisserie League champ. Without Rotisserie, there wouldn't have been "fantasy" sports, a booming market that some argue has helped substantially increase interest in professional sports.

continued on page 50

television sports wasn't in the habit of doing: tell a story."

But Arledge was not satisfied to simply capture the experience of a live game. He was determined to make televised sports a unique experience in its own right. Near the end of his historic memo, almost as an afterthought, he announced his intention of using video recorders to "replay the decisive plays of the first half [during] the halftime break." This, too, was a cutting-edge idea. Videorecording had been introduced in television just five years earlier and was still cumbersome to use. Finding the pictures you wanted, let alone editing the material for broadcast, was a chore. It offered no hope of anything like instant replay and no one had yet proposed using the equipment to bring slow-motion flashbacks to TV sports.

But Arledge did—that was his second epiphany. While visiting Tokyo in 1961, he decided to take in a samurai flick. He had no idea what the movie was about, but a slow-motion fight scene mesmerized him. "What if we could do the same in football?" he mused. "We could view the whole game differently." The technology hadn't been developed yet, but Arledge found an ABC engineer named Bob Trachinger who was willing to have a go at it. Trachinger came up with a crude system that required the action to be videotaped, then played onto a particular type of camera tube, while another camera retaped it at half speed. It took Trachinger about three months to produce a satisfactory slow-motion image—quite an achievement, since his ABC bosses regarded this work as a waste of time and took away his funding. (The innovative Ampex company was simultaneously developing "instant replay," but the public wouldn't see it until 1965 on CBS). Arledge debuted the technology later that year, at first with mixed results. But in a December contest between Boston College and Syracuse, slo-mo came into its own. In the first half, BC quarterback Jack Concannon took the ball on a magnificent 70-yard run, threading his way through the Syracuse defense for the score. At halftime, "we showed Concannon scoring in slo-mo," wrote Arledge, "with dreamlike grace this time, Paul Christman explaining every juke and jink. Watching, I saw the future open up before me."

Ed Sabol hated the garment business—especially the overcoats he'd spent almost 20 years selling. What he loved was movies. "He got his first movie camera as a wedding present in 1942," remembers his son, Steve Sabol. "Seemed like there was always a movie camera where his head was supposed to be. Growing up, I was never really sure he *had* a head, because he was always filming me." In 1962, Ed finally decided he had sold enough overcoats to start a film company: Blair Motion Pictures. Somehow, he wangled a grant to make a documentary about whales. "It was going to be called *To Catch a Whale*," Steve remembers. "What a *disaster*." Ed went to sea with a small camera crew, but became hopelessly seasick and his equipment was drenched with salt water. He never saw a whale. A lesser man might have given up. But just in time, Ed heard tell that exclusive filming rights to the 1961 NFL Championship had been purchased by closed bid from the commissioner's office for only $1,500. Ed knew that the price was way too low. For years, he had filmed his son's football games (Steve was, at the time, a running back at Colorado College) and he knew that football was loaded with drama. "He told me he was going to use football to tell a story, the way Hollywood told a story," says Steve. He also came up with $3,000 to be sure he won the bid.

NFL Commissioner Pete Rozelle was delighted that an unknown filmmaker was willing to pay double what he expected for the rights to film the 1962 Championship. But he blanched when he looked at Ed's résumé, which frankly admitted that his experience filming sports consisted entirely of filming his teenage son. Still, 3,000 bucks was 3,000 bucks, and Ed got his chance. He called his son and urged Steve to leave college. "He pointed out that all I was doing was playing football and going to the movies anyway, which meant I was perfectly qualified to work for him." Steve listened to his father's Hollywood strategy without much enthusiasm. "I wanted him to show the game the way I knew it as a player: muscles straining, eyeballs popping, jerseys tearing. We decided to put our two approaches together."

The '62 championship between Bart Starr's Packers and Y. A. Tittle's Giants turned out to be one of the most brutal football games ever played. The freezing Yankee Stadium turf was as rough and hard as rock salt. The weather was so cold that, on the sidelines, players emptied out water buckets, crumpled up pieces of paper and set them on fire, wiggling their fingers over the flames. It was an excruciating 16-7 Packer victory, and you could feel the pain and violence of each hit in the Sabols' 30-minute highlight film. One of their cameramen suffered such severe frostbite he lost the tips of two fingers. The whole tableau

"I'm not allowed to comment on lousy officiating."

—Jim Finks, New Orleans Saints GM, when asked after a loss what he thought of the refs

From haberdashery to smashmouthery *Ed Sabol was always a nice Jewish boy—but a discontented one, until he escaped the rag trade and found happiness as founding director of NFL Films.*

continued from page 48

7. Retractable roofs

The idea of a dome is simple: to keep the weather out. The idea of a retractable roof is beautiful: to keep the bad weather out, to let the good weather in. The first dome with a working retractable roof opened in Toronto in 1989. Domes with working retractable roofs are now in Seattle, Houston, Phoenix and Milwaukee.

8. Four-on-four OT in the NHL

Introduced in the 1999–2000 season, four-on-four (plus a goalie) opened up the ice and was designed to increase the possibility of a team breaking the deadlock. Previously, teams that remained tied at the end of a five-minute OT each got one point in the standings. With the new rule, teams that score in OT get an extra point.

9. Interleague play in baseball

There's a lot of debate about whether interleague play, introduced in 1997 during the regular season, is a good or bad thing. Some nattering nabobs of negativism point to phony rivalries invented to boost interest, or to the unfairness of an unbalanced schedule. But here's what's good: Every year, for a few weeks, fans get to see players they would otherwise see only in the postseason, if at all, and they get to see them in person, at regular prices. And some matchups are instant classics.

10. OPS and other "sabermetric" stats

Way back in the 1950s, Branch Rickey was telling the world (in *Life* magazine, no less) that batting average was overrated as an offensive statistic and that there were better ways to measure a player's offensive contributions. Thanks mostly to Bill James, we now have ways to evaluate players that are much better than they were 25 years ago. Old stats like on-base percentage have risen in prominence, new stats like OPS (on-base percentage + slugging percentage) provide new, simple measurements that take both power and the ability to draw walks into account. If baseball is an island of action surrounded by a sea of statistics, then the new stats have replenished the sea to the game's benefit.

reminded Ed of Normandy, where he'd served in World War II, and he called his film, unofficially, *Football's Longest Day*.

The Sabols' work was an order of magnitude better than any NFL highlight reel that preceded it. That's not saying much: According to Steve, only six of the era's teams bothered to film highlights at all, and of those, half were filmed by amateurs. No one thought of putting highlights on television. You'd show them at Kiwanis Clubs and Cub Scout meetings and the like for whatever money you could get. But the Sabols changed all of that, and after the 1964 season, each owner put up $20,000 to buy out Ed and put him to work as head of NFL Films. This operation was responsible for filming highlights from each and every game and, in the next few years, the Sabols used their monopoly to come up with a host of highlight innovations, including reverse-angle replays, miked coaches and, in 1967, perhaps the most important of all: a goofy five-minute reel of football bloopers called *The Headcracker Suite*. The NFL's first "follies" flick was met with all the enthusiasm one might expect from the notoriously humorless league office. "This is a *disgrace!*" roared Bob Cochran, the NFL's chief of broadcasting. "You cannot show this!" But Rozelle was more circumspect. He seemed to chuckle as he watched the reel and told the Sabols that if it was okay with the players, it was okay. "So we went up to the Eagles training camp and set up a projector in the cafeteria," recalls Steve. "The Eagles were awful at the time, so they were in that film a lot. In fact, Norm Snead, Jim Hill and Jack Concannon were all featured prominently. But they all loved it."

It was only a matter of time before the Sabols' work came to the attention of Roone Arledge, who featured it at halftime on his new *Monday Night Football* show, which debuted in September of 1970. Howard Cosell—who would one day top a *TV Guide* poll as both the nation's best-liked AND most-hated sportscaster—presented them with what he once called "the spontaneity of articulation that I possess." Looking back, it is hard to comprehend why anyone would willingly subject themselves to it. But at the time, "it was both a highlight breakthrough and a real attraction of *Monday Night Football*," says Michael Hiestand, who covers sports media for *USA Today*. "People were amazed that they could see all the Sunday games."

And yet, the nation's appetite for highlights had barely been whetted. True, there were highlights nightly on the local sports report, but it is almost impossible for a 21st-century

Football's longest day Sabol's stark, beautiful highlight reel of the NFL's 1962 Championship Game between the Packers and Giants helped convince NFL owners that good highlights could be good for business.

Warner Time
Warner Wolf taught a generation of New York sports-casters the right way to do highlights and the wrong way to style their hair.

sports fan to imagine how ragged they were. In those days, sports was considered the bastard child of the evening news—dead last in the batting order, even on the slowest news days. Only males were thought to care about sports, and not the most discerning ones, either, while *everyone* cared about the weather. So a law evolved among TV producers: "Need some extra time for a story? Any story at all? *Take it outta sports!*"

Given these conditions, it was incredible that highlights weren't much worse. "You had to shoot 'em yourself," recalls Warner Wolf, longtime anchor of New York's CBS affiliate. "We'd take a camera into the press room, and I'd have to tell the cameraman where the ball was going. He'd point it at the pitcher and follow the ball to the hitter, but if it was hit, I'd shout, 'Third base! Cut to third!' Phew, it was fun. But we usually had to leave after the fourth inning. We shot film in those days, so we had to rush back to get it developed."

It took a special kind of chutzpah to do highlights in those days, and Wolf, son of vaudevillians, had it. Never mind bumpy camera work; never mind that the best action had occurred after he and his camera had left the game; never mind that his three-minute sports report had been trimmed to two minutes, then trimmed again to 90 seconds. He'd tease the audience with a "Wait'll you see this!" tone of voice, twirl his finger like a magician and shout: "Let's go to the videotape!"

That's how it was done in the dark ages, known in the television business as "B.C."—before cable. ■

CHAPTER 3

If You're a Fan...

IKE ANY MAN OF IDEAS, BILL RASMUSSEN WAS USED TO being laughed at. He even had a rule: "When people laugh at you, maintain your confidence. Those people will soon discover that you were right." That was Bill—full of old-fashioned moxie, gusto and vim. Smart, too, no question about that. But—how to put it?—at 45, Bill did not appear destined to accomplish anything that historians would ever need to write down. In May of 1978, he looked as if his best years were behind him: hairline drifting out with the tide, crow's feet around his eyes, the skin beneath his chin just starting to droop. True, when he smiled, it was usually a big, mouthful-of-teeth smile; but right now, he had little to smile about. He had just been fired as communications director for the World Hockey Association's Hartford Whalers. But it took no more than a week for Bill Rasmussen to come up with the most laughable idea he'd ever had.

It came to him in a relaxed meeting with his future partners: his son Scott; an insurance agent named Ed Eagan; and a freelance TV producer named Bob Beyus. It was just the essence of an idea, really—*an idea for an idea*. If you could convince a few local sports teams—say, the UConn Huskies— to let you air their games on cable television then . . . well, maybe people would watch. It was impossible to predict much beyond that, because, in those days, there were just 14 mil-

Sports Heaven Anchors George Grande and Lee Leonard host the inaugural SportsCenter *on Septembert 7, 1979.*

"Football combines the two worst features of American life: **violence** and **committee meetings."**

—George Will, political commentator

lion cable subscribers scattered throughout the U.S. And most of those were hooked up not to receive any special programming (there was no CNN yet, no MTV), but because they happened to live near some large annoyance, like a mountain, which screwed up their aerial reception. People who thought of themselves as "technology experts" were still arguing in the *Wall Street Journal* about what cable technology was destined to become, if anything.

But Rasmussen didn't care about that—not yet. It was the little germ of an idea that excited him and he needed a name for it. He started with: "Eastern Sports Programming Network." For short, Rasmussen liked to call it the E.S.P. Network, because the double entendre made him chuckle. After a couple of weeks, he excitedly invited 35 Connecticut journalists to a press conference at a Holiday Inn, to unveil E.S.P. to the public. Only three reporters showed up, and they all laughed at him—especially when he admitted that he had no equipment, no customers and no permission to show any UConn football games that happened to fall on a Saturday. Bob Beyus was so humiliated by the experience that he dropped out of the venture that very night.

Boy with a toy Bill Rasmussen, shortly after his dreams came true.

Rasmussen maintained his confidence. People would soon see that he was right. He knew almost nothing about cable, but was intrigued to learn that satellites were involved. Apparently, you sent your broadcast signal from a satellite dish (or "uplink") to some satellite gizmo (or "transponder"), which then shot your signal over the entire country so it could be broadcast by any cable operator who wanted it. The fact that Rasmussen had no money to speak of did not stop him from meeting with RCA to see how much a transponder would cost to lease. The answer, $35,000 a month, seemed like rather a lot to spend just to broadcast tape-delayed UConn Huskies games. Had Rasmussen been an ordinary person, he would have immediately started looking for a cheaper, far more modest way of making his little dream a reality. But being Rasmussen, he did exactly the opposite: He supersized his dream. He would broadcast NCAA sports from *all over the country!* ESPN morphed into the "Entertainment and Sports Network" and became a kind of snowball, rolling down a hill, growing larger and larger as new ideas clung to it. It is still rolling to this day.

In order to bring ESPN to life, Rasmussen set off on a Bilbo Baggins sort of entrepreneurial odyssey. Theoretically, there was no way he could succeed: He needed investors; but to get investors, he needed an agreement with the NCAA that would allow him to show games on tape delay; but the NCAA wouldn't do business with him unless he had investors. At the same time, he had to convince advertisers to spend actual money for time on a hypothetical network, and he needed an actual building for his hypothetical offices and studios.

If you buy it, they will come
For $18,000, Bill Rasmussen purchased a small piece of Connecticut and a sign. Were it not for his savvy and salesmanship, the whole enterprise would have ended right there.

For $18,000, which he didn't exactly have, he convinced the bucolic town of Bristol, Connecticut (a place equally inconvenient from both New York and Boston), to sell him an acre of undeveloped land. It was like juggling snakes—investors, advertisers, NCAA, RCA, Bristol—writhing and hissing and snapping at him. Drop any one snake and the whole deal would be poisoned. As he struggled to keep them airborne, *everyone* seemed to be laughing at him. That is, until February of 1979, when Getty Oil purchased 85 percent of Rasmussen's idea for $10 million. Suddenly, all of the laughing stopped, cold; for everyone could see that Bill Rasmussen had been right all along.

Highlights were the last thing on anyone's mind as ESPN prepared for blastoff at 7 P.M., September 7, 1979. When the clock struck noon on that day, absolutely nothing was ready. The Bristol offices weren't finished, so the five dozen or so employees were installed in three trailers, which could be entered only by means of rickety stepladders treacherously planted in soupy mud. The studio wasn't finished, the set wasn't finished and much of the video equipment hadn't arrived. There weren't even any flushing toilets, just Porta Potties that attracted swarms of flies.

This ragtag operation was under the capable leadership of Chet Simmons, former president of NBC Sports. One of the first sportscasters Simmons hired was Lee Leonard, a guy who, if

"It's not how **good** you are when you **play good.** It's how good you are when you **play bad.** And we played pretty good, even though we played bad. **Imagine** if we'd **played good.**"

—Georgia guard Litterial Green after his team beat rival Georgia Tech, 66-65

> **"Even Jesus had trouble with 12 guys."**
> —Ex-Utah Jazz coach Frank Layden

Summer of '79, Rasmussen and company president Chet Simmons break ground at the future home of ESPN. As construction commenced at a frantic pace, Rasmussen's home (below) overflowed with video equipment that had nowhere else to stay.

he'd had his druthers, would have been hosting a talk show (and in a couple of years, he'd have one on CNN). He never pretended to be an expert on sports. "As far as I'm concerned," he liked to say, "they're a bunch of big guys in short pants making way too much money." This attitude helped make him unflappable as host of New York City's popular *SportsExtra* program, and later, NBC's *Grandstand*. He had a gift for improvisation, too, that ESPN would sorely need in the rickety months ahead.

Leonard knew that he'd be called upon to host a show called *SportsCenter*, but no one had time yet to think much about what the program would be. The idea of airing even one half-hour sports show, every single day, was unprecedented—where would you find enough material to fill it? Besides, everyone assumed that ESPN would stand or fall on the basis of three things: "Events, events, events," Leonard says. "That's all anyone talked about." *SportsCenter* would fill the empty hours in between those events—"kind of like spackle," as producer/director Bill Shanahan put it.

It wasn't until the morning of September 7 that a hasty meeting was finally assembled to determine *SportsCenter*'s content. Producer Bob Pronovost stood in front of a perfectly blank whiteboard, looking at a roomful of equally blank faces. Since there would be four commercial breaks, he drew four lines on the whiteboard and numbered them. Not one person in the room had any idea how the spaces in between would be filled. So Pronovost began firing questions, and slowly the answers began to come. It was September, so they'd lead with baseball scores. And what else?

Well, someone said: "What about highlights?"

"Truly, I don't believe anyone thought about highlights until that meeting," says Shanahan. "Certainly, no one had thought about where we might get them, because I remember somebody immediately ran down to the engineers to see what we could do." (Not much, apparently: When anchor George

Grande introduced the program later that evening, he promised a rosy future of scores, updates, interviews, and commentary—but not one word about highlights.)

In the meantime, there was the launch to think of. The studio was patched together by construction workers at the last minute, and Leonard and Grande were seated before a hokey-looking but expensive set, decorated with a menagerie of athletes dashing off in different directions to play different sports. The control room, however, was still uninhabitable, so a mobile TV truck was rented from a nearby public television station. It was a terrifying place to find yourself on September 7, that truck. Shanahan was floor producer and wore a headset that allowed him to hear everything that went on. The bickering was enough to burn your stomach. As 7 P.M. drew nearer, the colloquy devolved into "one long *unbelievable* string of obscenities," he says, still impressed after all these years. When Leonard tried to ask him a question, Shanahan answered by lifting the foul-mouthed earphones from his head so Leonard could hear the swearing. Leonard decided to save his question for another time.

And then, miraculously, 7 P.M. came and everything worked. The ESPN logo appeared, and with it, the new ESPN theme song, destined for a quick and most unlamented death, but right now, playing loud, brassy and clear:

Look us up and check us out, 'cause we're the one worth watchin'!
Total sports and en-ter-tain-ment, we're the one worth watchin'!
Yes, at a glance you'll recognize
The fact that we do specialize
We're total sports and entertainment!
E! S! P! N!
Everything worth see-in'!

Glory days In its first year, ESPN's production staff worked without benefit of private desks, days off or flushing toilets. The Porta Potties outside attracted swarms of flies, which often found their way into the studio, occasionally landing on an anchor's nose.

"**Sportswriters** are probably the only individuals in our universe who actually have less constructive jobs than I do. I don't do nothing but hit people. And they don't do nothing but talk about what I do."
—former heavyweight boxer Randall 'Tex' Cobb

> "My position is that while the **players don't deserve** all that **money,** the owners **don't deserve** it even more."
>
> —Jim Bouton

Leonard then gave an extemporaneous introduction that was so perfect for the occasion, it remains etched in TV history. He had planned to use the old Al Jolson line "You ain't heard nothin' yet!" but changed his mind at the last minute because, in this case, it was too true. Instead, he summed up Rasmussen's grandiose vision, and its intended audience, in just a few words. "If you're a fan," he began. Then he paused for just a beat and said it again: "*If* you're a fan"—seeming to imply that not every fan was fan enough to handle a station like ESPN. And he wanted those who might not be up to it to have a chance to run away, right now, like little wussies, and watch *M*A*S*H*. For those who remained, he continued: "What you'll see in the next minutes, hours and days to follow may convince you, you've gone to *sports heaven*."

Alas, there were still problems in sports heaven. "I'd watched the sign-on show and, boy, it was rugged," says Bob Ley, then a young anchor who was scheduled to start at ESPN two nights later. He meant that the sound had been absent for a live interview with University of Colorado football coach Chuck Fairbanks. (Someone nervously warned Leonard that, unless it came back, he might need to do some play-by-play later in the evening. "Certainly," Leonard replied cheerfully. "You just tell me who's in the dark shirts and who's in the white shirts, and I'll be glad to do it.") Ley, who had turned down a respectable public television gig to work at ESPN ("I thought it might be exciting"), was a little unnerved as he drove up the unpaved parking lot and walked inside the control room. There were pizza boxes strewn everywhere and flies buzzing around the set. "Oh, my God!" he thought to himself. "Did I trade an actual *job* for *this*?" A moment later, he was shaking hands with Alan B. "Scotty" Connal, a veteran producer whom Simmons had brought with him from NBC. Connal looked as if he hadn't slept since the Spanish-American War, but he waved at a TV monitor and said, "Look! We're on the air."

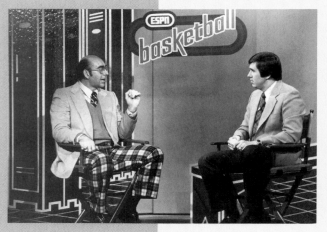

*"Smell the leather, babeee . . . "
Dick Vitale, his legs wrapped in a tablecloth, breaks down college hoops with Bob Ley in 1981. NCAA Tournament coverage was key to putting the upstart network on the map.*

"He said it with such *pride*, you know?" says Ley, and pride is infectious. "I'd never anchored a newscast in my life, but I sat down and did sixteen hours, including two *SportsCenters*—and I couldn't tell you how many sixteen-hour days would follow." Nor can he articulate what it was like to be an anchor in those early days, with acres of airtime to fill between events like Munster hurling (not Herman Munster tossing, unfortunately, but a kind of Irish field hockey) and the Slo-Pitch Softball All-Star Game. A few minutes of high-light video was a godsend, just to get the anchors' faces off the screen. But with a small staff and little money to spend, where would the material come from?

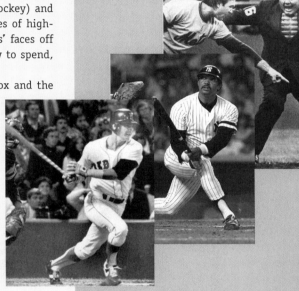

"Most of our highlights were from the Red Sox and the Yankees and the Mets and the Red Sox and the Yankees and the Mets," says Ley. "See a pattern there? They were local, so we could tape them right off the set. We'd try to get freelancers to film some for us, but that didn't always work. We're still waiting for the 1979 Grey Cup high-lights to show up. They were supposed to arrive by bus. And you know what really hurts? That freelancer got paid."

Outsiders were not to be trusted. Instead, snagging highlights became one of the chief pas-sions of the young staff. "It was like Dodge City," says producer Fred Muzzy. "No one had ever done anything like it before, so there were no rules." Well, actual-ly, there were rules, but they were pretty much ignored by the cowboys at ESPN. "There were gray areas about what games you could use and how you could use them," says Muzzy. "Who owned the rights? Could you tape it and show high-lights? The answers were often complicated. For instance, you could use NFL stuff, but only twenty-four to forty-eight hours after the game, otherwise you had to pay by the second. You could show other highlights, but not until the game was over. So . . ."

"So, we started cheating a little bit," says Leonard. "We'd use a little more than we were supposed to, and then maybe a little more . . ."

"And then we'd get a call from someone upstairs," says Muzzy. "Because maybe CBS was complaining that we were using too much of their stuff and we had to stop. So we'd stop. For a while. Then we'd start up again."

Triptych *If you were an ESPN viewer in the early '80s, you saw an awful lot of highlights involving three teams— the three that just happened to be on local TV in Bristol, Connecticut.*

■ There was always potential for good sports movies—conflict and drama and comedy, the staples of Hollywood, are built into the games we play. In 1973, we saw some of the possibilities with *Bang the Drum Slowly*, but *Rocky*, which premiered on November 21, 1976, opened the floodgates. It grossed hundreds of millions and gave us some great catchphrases ("Yo! Adrian!" and "Women weaken legs!" for example). The secret to the great sports movies of the past 25 years? Good scripts, from which come memorable lines, the ones that are instantly recognizable: You need more of an explanation? Show me the money.

■ ■ ■

"Don't try to strike everybody out. Strikeouts are boring and besides that, they're fascist. Throw some ground balls. They're more democratic."

—*Crash Davis (Kevin Costner) to Nuke LaLoosh (Tim Robbins) in* **Bull Durham** (1988)

■

"I believe in the soul . . . the small of a woman's back, the hanging curveball, high fiber, good scotch, that the novels of Susan Sontag are self-indulgent, overrated crap. I believe Lee Harvey Oswald acted alone. I believe there ought to be a constitutional amendment outlawing Astroturf and

the designated hitter. I believe in the sweet spot, soft-core pornography, opening your presents Christmas morning rather than Christmas Eve, and I believe in long, slow, deep, soft, wet kisses that last three days."

—*Crash Davis (Kevin Costner) in* **Bull Durham** (1988)

■

Batboy (Tobi Eshelman): "Get a hit, Crash."

Crash Davis (Kevin Costner): "Shut up."

—**Bull Durham** (1988)

■ ■ ■

Jimmy Dugan (Tom Hanks): "Shit, Dottie, if you want to go back to Oregon and make a hundred babies, great, I'm in no position to tell anyone how to live. But sneaking out like this, quitting, you'll regret it for the rest of your life. Baseball is what gets inside you. It's what lights you up, you can't deny that."

Dottie Hinson (Geena Davis): "It just got too hard."

Dugan: "It's supposed to be hard! If it wasn't hard, everyone would do it. The hard . . . is what makes it great!"

—**A League of Their Own** (1992)

■

Jimmy Dugan (Tom Hanks): "Evelyn, could you come here for a second? Which team do you play for?"

Evelyn Gardner (Bitty Schram): "Well, I'm a Peach."

Dugan: "Well, I was just wonderin' why you would throw home when we got a two-run lead! You let the tying run get

on second base and we lost the lead because of you! Start using your head. That's the lump that's three feet above your ass!"

[Evelyn starts to cry.]

"Are you crying? Are you crying? Are you crying? There's no crying, there's no crying in baseball! Rogers Hornsby was my manager, and he called me a talking pile of pigshit! And that was when my parents drove all the way down from Michigan to see me play the game! And did I cry? NO! NO! And do you know why?"

Evelyn: "No, no, no."

Dugan: "Because there's no crying in baseball!"

—**A League of Their Own** (1992)

■ ■ ■

Maude Lebowski (Julianne Moore): "What do you do for recreation?"

The Dude (Jeff Bridges): "Oh, the usual. I bowl. Drive around. The occasional acid flashback."

—**The Big Lebowski** (1998)

■ ■ ■

Willie Mays Hayes (Wesley Snipes): "I'm Willie Mays Hayes. I hit like Mays, and I run like Hayes."

Lou Brown (James Gammon): "Well, you may run like Mays, but you hit like shit."

—**Major League** (1989)

■

"Juuuuuuust a bit outside."

—*Harry Doyle (Bob Uecker) in* **Major League** (1989)

■ ■ ■

"The price is wrong, bitch!"

—*Happy Gilmore (Adam Sandler) fighting with Bob Barker in* **Happy Gilmore** (1996)

"So I jump ship in Hong Kong and make my way over to Tibet, and I get on as a looper at a course over in the Himalayas. A looper, you know, a caddy, a looper, a jock. So, I tell them I'm a pro jock, and who do you think they give me? The Dalai Lama, himself. Twelfth son of the Lama. The flowing robes, the grace, bald . . . striking. So, I'm on the first tee with him. I give him the driver. He hauls off and whacks one—big hitter, the Lama—long, into a 10,000-foot crevasse, right at the base of this glacier. Do you know what the Lama says? Gunga galunga . . . gunga, gunga-galunga. So we finish the 18th and he's gonna stiff me. And I say, 'Hey, Lama, hey, how about a little something, you know, for the effort, you know?' And he says, 'Oh, uh, there won't be any money, but when you die, on your deathbed, you will receive total consciousness.' So I got that goin' for me, which is nice."

> —*Carl Spackler (Bill Murray) in*
> ***Caddyshack*** (1980)

"The one constant through all the years has been baseball. America has rolled by like an army of steamrollers. It's been erased like a blackboard, rebuilt, and erased again. But baseball has marked the time. This field, this game, is a part of our past. It reminds us of all that once was good, and what could be again."

> —*Terence Mann (James Earl Jones) in*
> ***Field of Dreams*** (1989)

"If you build it, they will come."

> —*The Voice (uncredited) in*
> ***Field of Dreams*** (1989)

"Sex and golf are the two things you can enjoy even if you're not good at them."

> —*Roy McAvoy (Kevin Costner) in*
> ***Tin Cup*** (1996)

"Show me the money!"

> —*Rod Tidwell (Cuba Gooding Jr.) in*
> ***Jerry Maguire*** (1996)

"Pain heals. Chicks dig scars. Glory lasts forever."

> —*Shane Falco (Keanu Reeves) in*
> ***The Replacements*** (2000)

"Shut your anorexic, malnutrition, tapeworm-havin', overdosin'-on-Dick-Gregory's-Bahamian-Diet ass up!"

> —*Sidney Deane (Wesley Snipes) in*
> ***White Men Can't Jump*** (1992)

Roy Hobbs (Robert Redford): "I coulda been better. I coulda broke every record in the book."

Iris Gaines (Glenn Close): "And then?"

Roy Hobbs: "And then? And then when I walked down the street people would've looked and they would've said there goes Roy Hobbs, the best there ever was in this game."

> —***The Natural*** (1984)

"You find out life's this game of inches, so is football. Because in either game—life or football—the margin for error is so small. I mean, one half a step too late or too early and you don't quite make it. One half second too slow, too fast and you don't quite catch it. The inches we need are everywhere around us. They're in every break of the game, every minute, every second. On this team, we fight for that inch. On this team, we tear ourselves and everyone else around us to pieces for that inch. We claw with our fingernails for that inch. Because we know when you add up all those inches, that's gonna make the f***ing difference between winning and losing! Between living and dying!"

> —*Tony D'Amato (Al Pacino) in*
> ***Any Given Sunday*** (1999)

Interviewer (Mario Machado): "What's your prediction for the fight?"

Clubber Lang (Mr. T): "My prediction? Pain."

> —***Rocky III*** (1982)

Rocky (Sylvester Stallone): "I see three of him out there."

Paulie (Burt Young): "Hit the one in the middle."

> —***Rocky IV*** (1985)

"If he wanted me to run 26 miles through hills, I would. If he wanted me to carry water bottles, I would. If he wanted me to get my hair cut like his . . . well, you have to draw the line somewhere."

—Cowboys backup QB Babe Laufenberg on Jimmy Johnson

The job of plundering whatever games were on the airwaves fell to a few production assistants, most of whom were sports freaks fresh out of college. Typically, they would position themselves in the corner of a little screening room and watch as many games as possible, simultaneously. "We'd try to guess which ones were likely to be the most important and concentrate on those," says Bob Rauscher, one of ESPN's first PAs and now senior coordinating producer of *NFL Primetime*. "But inevitably we'd guess wrong and an inconsequential baseball game where nothing much seemed to be happening would turn out to be a no-hitter." So the last few minutes before the show were always a mad scramble.

But that just contributed to the general sense of excitement, and fed the network's pride in its own ballsiness. "We were the naughty ones in the back of the class," says Ley, the little upstart network, taking on the Big Three. And so ESPN began to develop its unique point of view, a combination of reverence for sports and irreverence for every convention that pertained to sports. The unexpected highlight was always welcome, the ludicrous highlight even more so.

Baby Boomer A very young Chris Berman wih a fuzzy caterpillar creeping across his lips.

"We had some news service out of Europe," recalls Muzzy, by way of illustration. "I say we had it. I don't know if we had the rights to use it. But we loved it, because they would have, say, an auto race in Dakar, with cars going through the mud and natives throwing rocks. My favorite highlight, maybe of all time, was something they sent from Australia or New Zealand. It was a guy on a motorcycle who would drive into a brick wall, helmet-first. Off he'd go, and you'd hear this, 'ka-clink,' and then there'd be bricks flying around everywhere! We showed it over and over again."

It was a lot like anarchy, the more so since no one seemed to be watching—not even the brass who ran the network. "That's really what allowed us to flourish," says Shanahan. "Since ESPN was still event-driven, *SportsCenter* was considered, um, unglamorous."

"Unglamorous?" gasps Ley. "Management treated it like

a chinchilla farm, do you hear me? As far as they were concerned, *SportsCenter* chugged along like a case of athlete's foot in your sock."

Chris Berman arrived at the chinchilla farm in October of 1979. At 24, he looked like no sportscaster on television, with long hair and what he called a "Luis Tiant moustache," which, before long, he shrewdly removed. He could hardly believe that he was making $16,500 a year to cover sports, and though he'd "really battled for that $500," he'd have done it for far less.

A show about nothing ESPN easily obtained the rights to broadcast the NFL draft, because no one else wanted any part of it.

Berman's first assignment was to host the overnight *SportsCenter*, a program that may have been witnessed by no more than a few dozen insomniacs. The standard for highlights could scarcely have been lower. Since the majority of sports were broadcast only to local audiences, the only way to get video of far-flung games was to have tapes delivered by air freight. "If the weather was good at the Hartford airport, we'd get yesterday's highlights," says Berman. "If it was bad, they'd be from the day before yesterday. Either way, they went on the air."

Longing for something a little fresher, Berman would go out to games whenever he could, with a cameraman and a producer, to make highlights of his own. "If I had a few days off, they'd pay for half my ticket down to Tampa, and I'd pay the other half. I'd visit friends on Saturday, then go to the Bucs game on Sunday." In addition to filming the contest, he would interview players on every subject he could think of, knowing that he could use their answers in other highlight reels later on in the season. "Generally, the game ended at 4, the flight left Tampa at 8 and I'd land in Connecticut at 12:30 with three sound bites from Lee Roy Selmon, or whoever. We'd do a quick edit and pop 'em on the air." It wasn't much, but it was news and, more important, *news the networks didn't have*.

Over the next few years, ESPN elbowed its way into public awareness, first by presenting the entire NCAA basketball tournament, an event no one else wanted, and then with live

"**Sometimes they write what I say and not what I mean.**"

—Pedro Guerrero on sportswriters

Awe-Inspiring Nicknames

■ Sports nicknames have taken a real hit over the past quarter century—most have become mere abbreviations of names, much less creative than the substitute monikers of previous decades. But there are still some great ones, which provide a kind of shorthand for broadcasters who have to reel off 10 play descriptions in 10 seconds. Say "The Human Eraser" and everyone knows what's coming—a blocked shot, courtesy of Marvin Webster.

■ **"Round Mound of Rebound"**
Charles Barkley

■ **"Human Highlight Reel"**
Dominique Wilkins

■ **"Charlie Hustle"**
Pete Rose

■ **"Phi Slamma Jamma"**
The University of Houston men's basketball teams of 1982-'83 and '83-'84

■ **"Magic" Johnson**
Earvin Johnson

■ **"The Great One"**
Wayne Gretzky

■ **"The Human Rain Delay"**
Mike Hargrove

■ **"Sweetness"**
Walter Payton

■ **"The Big Hurt"**
Frank Thomas

coverage of the NFL draft, which no one else would have touched with a ten-foot goalpost. ("Nothing happens at a draft," says Dan Steir, now a coordinating producer, "so everyone thought we were crazy.")

But an equally seminal moment came in 1979, as Berman was narrating a set of routine baseball highlights. With no forethought ("none whatsoever," he insists), he bestowed a nickname on a baseball player. He can't remember today whether it was Frank Tanana Daiquiri or John Mayberry RFD. "Probably Tanana, because I used to do this kind of thing with my friends, while we were *drinking* Tanana Daiquiris." Immediately, the producer squawked in Berman's earphone: "*What?!*" Berman froze and noticed that the picture was hopping around the screen as the cameraman shook with laughter. He didn't realize what he'd said, had just blurted it naturally. "My first thought was, I must have used a swear word. In my mind, I went over George Carlin's list of things never to say on television, trying to figure out which one had slipped out."

What he'd actually done would prove as important as it was goofy, and shows that no act of creativity, however small, is ever wasted. The nicknames became a phenomenon. To be sure, the phenomenon took a few years to gather steam, like ESPN itself. The network, which had been available in only 1.4 million homes in 1979, arrived in five times that number of homes the following year, new nicknames pouring out all the while: Tom "Leave It to" Seaver, Bruce "Eggs" Benedict, Jamie "Men at" Quirk, Ross "I Never Promised You a" Baumgarten. By 1982, the number of subscribers had tripled again, surpassing 22 million. And that is when Berman's nicknames became a national craze, comparable to the hula hoop or the Macarena. It was, as baseball analyst Jerry "Rolls" Reuss once told Berman, a game everyone could play. Already popular inside ESPN, it spread like a virus among viewers (one of whom wrote in to suggest Ron "Born in the U.S." Cey), and, to Berman's shock, among players.

Still only 29, Berman was as much in awe of professional athletes as any sandlot kid. He couldn't believe it when the Kansas City Royals made a fuss over him shortly before a crucial playoff game against California. George Brett, one of Berman's all-time heroes, introduced himself as if there was no reason for Berman to know who he was. "Hi," he said, "I'm George Brett." Then he started ribbing Berman. "Hey, why

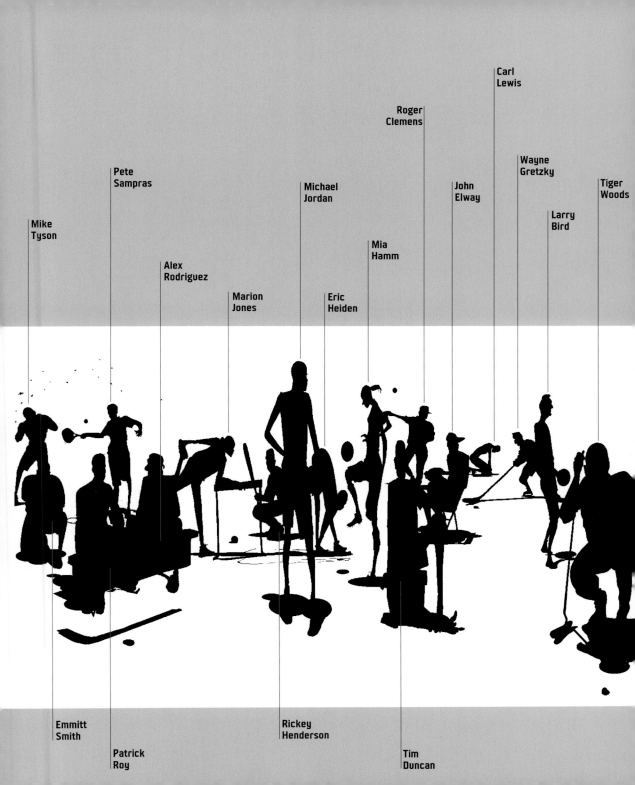

Carl
Lewis

Roger
Clemens

Pete
Sampras

Michael
Jordan

John
Elway

Wayne
Gretzky

Tiger
Woods

Mike
Tyson

Larry
Bird

Alex
Rodriguez

Mia
Hamm

Marion
Jones

Eric
Heiden

Emmitt
Smith

Rickey
Henderson

Patrick
Roy

Tim
Duncan

The ESPN Athletic Club

Where the 35 Greatest Athletes of the Last 25 Years Go When They Want to Be Alone Illustration by Istvan Banyai

Lance Armstrong

Cancer survivor. An American in France, whipping the Europeans at their own game. There's something "sweet" about that, and it keeps getting sweeter as the Tour victories keep piling up.

Larry Bird

The "hick from French Lick" turned the Celtics around immediately in his rookie year, led Boston to three titles in the 1980s, and, with rival and friend Magic Johnson, revived the NBA.

Barry Bonds

The only position player in baseball who changes entire games simply by his presence. The only great pro athlete to "peak" after turning 35. Regularly mentioned in the same sentence as Babe Ruth, which says more than any statistical accomplishment.

Roger Clemens

Another power pitcher from Texas, and the best of them all, thanks in part to his post–Red Sox years. The Bosox thought him washed up and expendable as he neared the end of his career, but they thought wrong, as Clemens picked up three more Cy Youngs—a record six in all—and a couple of rings with the Yankees. The best pitcher in baseball during the past 25 years.

Tim Duncan

Put Duncan right up there with Larry Bird, Elgin Baylor, Bob Pettit, and Oscar Robertson: they're the only five players in history to be named first-team All-NBA in their first six seasons. Also a two-time MVP and two-time NBA champion. And he's "just getting started."

Dale Earnhardt

"The Intimidator." "The Man in Black." "Ironhead." "No. 3." Earnhardt had plenty of monikers, but the adjective most used when describing the seven-time Winston Cup champ was "fearless." His death on the track at Daytona raised him into another realm, just as he transformed NASCAR into a national sport.

John Elway

He played in five Super Bowls, won two, threw for more than 50,000 yards in his 16 NFL seasons, and ran for more than 3,000 (not bad for a QB, huh?). When he hung up his cleats, he was simply the winningest QB in football history, with a 148-82-1 record.

Wayne Gretzky

The modest, classy No. 99 turned the obscure oil town of Edmonton into the hockey capital of the world in the 1980s, shattering all kinds of NHL goal-scoring and assists records. He'd go Hollywood and New York before it was all over, but the big-city hoopla didn't change The Great One.

Florence Griffith Joyner

Nobody's come close to FloJo's 100 meter world record of 10.49, set in the 1988 Olympic Trials. She also set a WR in the 200, which still stands. FloJo was a one-woman fashion show, but her legacy, after dying during an epileptic seizure at age 38, may always be tainted by rumors that she used performance-enhancing drugs.

Mia Hamm

Who would have believed, 25 years ago, that a female soccer player would soon become one of the most famous and respected athletes in the U.S.? Mia's more than a great soccer player, she's an icon.

Eric Heiden

February, 1980. Lake Placid, New York. Winter Olympics. Nine days. Five individual gold medals. Five Olympic medals. Not one for the limelight, he then switched sports and became, in 1985, the U.S. pro cycling champion.

Rickey Henderson

The Energizer Bunny of baseball, Rickey just keeps going and going and going. We won't forget all his career records—runs scored, steals, walks— for a long time. Nor will we forget how he talked about himself in the third person, creating a linguistic style that seems—for better or for worse—to be with us to stay.

Magic Johnson

Big smile. Incredible enthusiasm. His rivalry with Bird will never be forgotten. His leadership of the 1980s showtime Lakers seemed predestined. His 1991 announcement that he had been stricken with HIV—and his public life afterward—had a major influence for the good, not just on sports but on American culture.

Marion Jones

The mysterious "Mrs. Jones" featured in the classic Nike ads leading up to the 2000 Olympics was the complete package: Good looks, charm and wicked speed. She won her first championship in the 100 meters in 1997, and three years later everyone was asking: Would she win five gold medals in the Sydney Games? She ended up with "only" three golds and two bronzes.

Michael Jordan

When he was still in his 30s, still *playing*, they were building statues of His Airness. That's kind of strange, but for MJ, it was also fitting.

Jackie Joyner-Kersee

Named after Jackie Kennedy, Joyner-Kersee later fulfilled some kind of prophecy by becoming the First Lady of Track. She dominated the heptathlon, winning a silver medal at the 1984 games and then a gold in 1988 and 1992, and her marks have yet to be broken. Bruce Jenner put it simply: "She's the greatest multi-event athlete ever, man or woman."

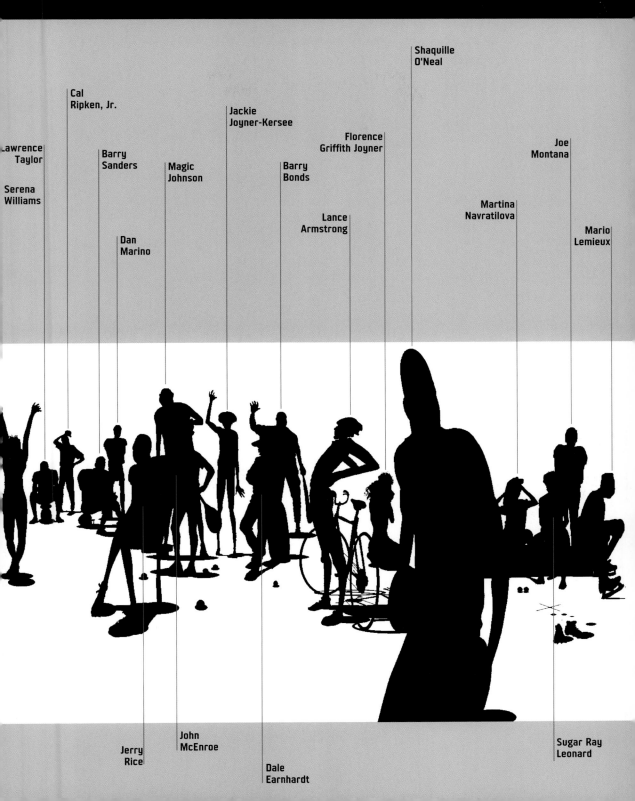

Shaquille
O'Neal

Cal
Ripken, Jr.

Jackie
Joyner-Kersee

Florence
Griffith Joyner

Lawrence
Taylor

Barry
Sanders

Magic
Johnson

Barry
Bonds

Joe
Montana

Serena
Williams

Martina
Navratilova

Dan
Marino

Lance
Armstrong

Mario
Lemieux

Jerry
Rice

John
McEnroe

Dale
Earnhardt

Sugar Ray
Leonard

Mario Lemieux

When he decided to wear No. 66 for the Penguins—Gretzky's 99, upside down—Lemieux set the bar pretty high for himself. Then he jumped over the bar, challenging Gretzky as the greatest point machine in NHL history. At the top of his game, he triumphed over Hodgkin's disease, retired young and was elected to the HOF, then bought the Penguins and returned to the ice more than three years after hanging up his skates. He hadn't lost it: In 2000-2001, he scored 76 points in just 43 games.

Sugar Ray Leonard

Sugar Ray was the first boxer to win more than $100 million in the ring, collecting championship belts in five weight classes. Cool and charismatic, fast and flashy, he picked up boxing's glamour torch from Muhammad Ali while engaging in classic bouts against Roberto Duran, Thomas Hearns and "Marvelous" Marvin Hagler.

Carl Lewis

He entered the national consciousness in 1984, when he won four golds in track and field at the 1984 Olympics. And then he stayed. In Seoul, in 1988, he became the only man ever to win back-to-back golds in the 100 and long jump. In 1992, he picked up two more golds. And in 1996, well past old-man status, he won the Olympic long jump an incredible fourth time in a row, bringing his lifetime gold medal total to nine. Never beloved, but undeniably great.

Dan Marino

Marino practically owns the NFL record book in passing, having thrown for about 35 *miles* during his 17 years with the Dolphins.

John McEnroe

Young and nasty and brash and so good. McEnroe, nicknamed "Superbrat" by the British press, played one of the greatest tennis matches of all time against Björn Borg in the 1980 Wimbledon final, ultimately losing in a marathon-length classic. But he'd eventually win Wimbledon, and even win hearts in England.

Joe Montana

He wasn't the strongest, or the fastest, or the biggest. He didn't have the best arm. He wasn't flashy. But he was, as *SI* put it, "The Ultimate Winner," having won four Super Bowls. Put it another way: in the fourth quarter with the game on the line, nobody did it better.

Martina Navratilova

She was different: a lefty, a lesbian, one of the first sports defectors from behind the Iron Curtain, and she played her best tennis after age 25, ultimately winning us over with her wins (nine Wimbledons, four U.S. Opens, three French Opens, two Aussie Opens), her smile and her great rivalry and friendship with Chris Evert.

Shaquille O'Neal

Don't get in his way. Off the court, Shaq's a sweetheart, but on the court, he's an enormous offensive dominator who pummels even the biggest of the NBA's big men. Now if only he could shoot free throws . . .

Jerry Rice

About midway through his career, the wide receiver from Mississippi Valley State began breaking NFL *career* records. The hardest working man in football crossed the Bay from SF to Oakland late in his career and continues to add big numbers to his NFL career marks in receptions, yards receiving, yards from scrimmage, all-purpose yards and TD receptions.

Cal Ripken, Jr.

Two words for you: Iron Man.

Alex Rodriguez

What's the perfect gift for the guy who has everything—unofficial "best player in the game" status, an MVP, $252 million contract, youth and good looks? Why, Yankee pin-stripes, of course.

Patrick Roy

The best goaltender in NHL history first led the Canadiens to two Stanley Cups, then the Colorado Avalanche to two more. "St. Patrick" perfected the "butterfly" style of goaltending, and his style and bravado raised the stature of all NHL goalies.

Pete Sampras

Just when sports fans (and sports writers) had gotten used to brash, cocky, outspoken, prima-donna superstars, along came Pete. They complained about the former, then they complained because Sampras was—as he became the best player in tennis history, while remaining true to his old self—quiet and unassuming.

Barry Sanders

In every single one of his 10 seasons with the Lions, Sanders was great. Maybe the best NFL back ever, Sanders, always publicity-shy, quietly walked away from the game in 1999, and has barely been heard from since.

Emmitt Smith

Smith became the leading rusher in NFL history, breaking Walter Payton's record, thanks to both great talent and incredible durability. Only 5-foot-9 and 199 pounds, Smith entered the NFL in 1990 and led the Cowboys to three Super Bowl wins. After he broke Payton's all-time rushing record, Eddie, Walter's brother, remarked, "[Walter] once said that if anybody breaks his record, he hopes it is Emmitt because he would do it with the class and the dignity that the record represents."

Lawrence Taylor

LT was a wild man, a dominating outside linebacker with all kinds of personal problems. But on the field, his speed, strength, leadership and intelligence did nothing less than change the way offenses played. One of the few defensive players to win the NFL MVP award (in 1986).

Mike Tyson

For a while, the former heavyweight was the "baddest man on the planet." And a decade into his downhill slide, he remains the biggest draw and the most fascinating spectacle in boxing.

Serena Williams

She plays, she styles and she's power-ful, a dominating presence in women's tennis like none before her.

Tiger Woods

Not only is Tiger the greatest *golfer* of the past 25 years, he's a great *athlete*: strong, agile, elegant, and—pun intended—eagle eyed.

don't the Royals have more nicknames?" Flabbergasted, Berman wasn't sure what to say. "What's *your* nickname?" Brett went on. Berman replied that he didn't have one, at least so far as he knew (his colleagues would eventually dub him "Boomer" on account of his reverberant baritone voice, which, according to one PA, "can loosen your fillings"). "Ha!" said the future Hall of Famer. "Come by my locker after the game, I'll have one for you."

Berman was flattered, but by the time the game had ended, he knew Brett would have far more important things on his mind. Hadn't he smacked the game-winning hit in the bottom of the eighth inning, leading KC to a 6-5 win? When Berman got to the locker room, Brett had emerged from the showers with a towel around his waist, enthusiastically reliving the game for a herd of scribbling reporters. Suddenly, he stopped in mid-sentence. "Aha! There he is!" Brett shouted. *"Ethel Merman* Berman!" The TV reporters were incensed, grumbling that Berman had spoiled their interview (they certainly weren't going to blame Brett). But Berman had made a friend for life, and that friendship would prove crucial to preserving ESPN's point of view.

SportsCenter, meanwhile, was surpassing all expectations. "We had an NFL show at noon on Sunday, a highlight merry-go-round, and there was no competition on the networks," says Muzzy. "We'd have tapes picked up from the airport—interviews with the players [about the day's games]—and they had to be screened and edited, and you never knew what you had until the last possible minute. But all the football fans were sitting at home with nothing to do, just waiting for the games to start. The show got ratings that were unheard of at ESPN in those days."

And yet, watching a *SportsCenter* from the mid-'80s is a strange experience. The show had much the same spirit as it does today, whether hosted by Ley, Berman, Gayle Gardner, Greg Gumbel, or the late Tom Mees. But while the number of highlights had increased exponentially since '79, it was still meager by today's standards. With more airtime than video, the hosts were often forced to blabber on well after they'd run out of things to say. A basketball game between North Carolina and Georgetown inevitably produced a windy debate on the relative merits of the ACC and Big East conferences. The announcers were "stretching"—that is, filling dead air—simply because they didn't have anything else to do. The pro-

- **"Cujo"**
Curtis Joseph

- **"The Answer"**
Allen Iverson

- **"The Human Eraser"**
Marvin Webster

- **"He Hate Me"**
Rod Smart

- **"The Iceman"**
George Gervin

- **"The Microwave"**
Vinnie Johnson

- **"Bake" McBride**
Arnold Ray McBride

- **"The Big Unit"**
Randy Johnson

- **"Oil Can" Boyd**
Dennis Boyd

- **"Air" Jordan**
Michael Jordan

- **"Chocolate Thunder"**
Darryl Dawkins

- **"Dr. Dunkenstein"**
Darrell Griffith

- **"The Doctor"**
Julius Erving

- **"The Mailman"**
Karl Malone

- **"The Glove"**
Gary Payton

- **"The Wizard of Oz"**
Ozzie Smith

Royal protector *The great George Brett stood up for Chris Berman's right to make up nicknames—and helped preserve ESPN's irreverent identity.*

"I'll always be Number 1 to myself."
—Moses Malone

gram could certainly be improved. The question was, how to improve it? Should it strive to be more informative, more entertaining, or both?

In June of 1984, just as this debate began to get an airing, a corporate bomb fell from the sky: ABC purchased ESPN for somewhere around one quarter of one billion dollars.

There's no need to point fingers about what happened next. Best to say that it took time for a large corporation to appreciate the village culture of the small one. It was, after all, that small-town culture that had made ESPN worth so much of ABC's money. After five years of nearly unfettered creativity, edicts were suddenly handed down from above and employees judged mainly on their ability to carry those edicts out. The clash of cultures reached its nadir when an executive called Berman into his office and ordered him to knock off the nicknames.

As bad corporate decisions go, this one ranked with the Edsel, "New Coke" and Time Warner's purchase of AOL. At first, all Berman could do was gasp: "Why?"

"We need to broaden our audience," he was told.

"But that's just what the nicknames do!" he argued. "People may not like sports, but when they hear Von 'Purple' Hayes, they laugh. I know, because they've told me!"

This may have been true, but it was the wrong answer, and Berman was made to understand it. People were being fired all around him, and there was nothing unfirable about him. He begged for permission to use the nicknames just until the end of the season, but that permission was denied. So he bit his lip and did what he was told. Sort of.

At first, he tried using no nicknames whatsoever, referring to "the Babe" only as George Herman Ruth; to "Sparky" as George Lee Anderson; and to "Whitey" as Dorrel Norman Elvert Herzog. No one cared. Beaten, he called his friend George Brett to wish him the best of luck as the season drew to a close. He apologized for abandoning the nicknames and explained the situation. Brett told him to cheer up.

In the fall of 1985, George Grande went to Toronto to cover the American League Championship Series. It was the Royals' year, for they were destined to win it all behind the brilliant pitching of Bret Saberhagen. Grande sought out Brett for an interview, and Brett seemed to wait for just the right accumulation of reporters before bawling: "George, what happened to the nicknames? Is it true they're not letting Chris use 'em anymore?" Grande replied that it was, and all hell broke loose. *USA Today* ran the news and the *Los Angeles Times*, which had regularly published lists of Berman's nicknames, phoned the network, demanding to know why Berman was being censored.

"We're not censoring Chris," an executive tried to explain. "We're only asking Chris to moderate his use of nicknames." (This was news to Berman.) "We want to establish *SportsCenter* as a show of record, and we don't think nicknames fit in with hard, Page 1 sports news."

Berman admitted to the *L.A. Times* that it was "kind of hard getting used to. Jose Cruz hit a homer on the last day of the season. To me, it's Jose 'Can You See' Cruz. When I said his name, there was a three-second break between Jose and Cruz. I really had to catch myself."

Letters of protest poured in from viewers. It was such a small matter . . . and yet it wasn't. It was as if a good friend of yours, whose jokes always gave you a snicker, had been told by a bully to shut the hell up. Worse, it seemed like an attempt to sanitize a voice that was refreshingly human. Berman, in a word, seemed to have the world in proper perspective; his bosses did not. It wasn't long before Berman found himself with new bosses.

But *SportsCenter* still needed a makeover. And the highlights—even with Jesse "Belly Up to the" Barfield hitting against Bert "Be Home" Blyleven—were all starting to look the same. ■

■ **ESPN has pulled the plug** on Chris Berman's baseball player nicknames.

No more Ron (Born In the U.S.) Cey. No more Frank Tanana Daiquiri, Dave Righetti and Meatballs or Glen (Mother) Hubbard. No more John (Tonight, Let It Be) Lowenstein or Rick (Innocent) Lysander.

Berman, one of the anchors on ESPN's "SportsCenter" show, has used more than 200 nicknames on the air since 1979.

Deciding that they must go was Jack Gallivan, who became executive producer of "SportsCenter" a few months ago. He told Berman last week.

Los Angeles Times, *October 11, 1985*

"He's a quick learner, but he forgets quick, too."
—Mychal Thompson on center Vlade Divac

67

CHAPTER 4

Reinventing the Reel

HE HIGHLIGHTS ALL LOOKED THE SAME BECAUSE, STRUC-
turally, most of them *were* the same, representing a
single genre, or approach: the Who Won? highlight.
This genre, also known as the Chronological highlight,
consists of a straightforward recap of a game's pivotal
moments, beginning with the first inning (or quarter, or
round, or period, or set) and ending with the last. One wag
calls it the "'Great-day-for-a-ballgame' 'Holy cow, what a
play!' 'Backbackbackback—outta here!' 'That'll be a web gem'
'. . . and-*makes*-the-catch-for-the-final-out'" highlight. Start
with the beginning, put the middle in the middle, end with
the end.

Mind you, this is not said with any disrespect. No one at
ESPN would *dare* disrespect the Who Won? highlight, any more
than a poet would disrespect the sonnet, or a boxer would disrespect the jab. True, the Who Won? may seem passé now that
ESPN has invented an infinite variety of zany approaches to
telling the story of a sporting event. In recent years, there
have been highlights in the form of mock restaurant reviews
("Cuban's House of Hoops" was said to be a diner in Dallas
where visitors were served huge portions of "Nowitzki
Schnitzel" and "Nash Canadian Bacon"). There have been
rhyming basketball highlights, including a Dr. Seussian reel
called "Big Dog and Ham." ("Sam-I-Am with the rock, he

Beantown breakthrough ESPN's legendary "Boston Massacre" highlight
conveyed all the vicissitudes of a moody city on an emotional day—setting
a new, ambitious standard for the craft.

"People think we make **$3 million** and **$4 million** a year. They don't realize that most of us **only** make **$500,000.**"

—Pete Incaviglia, baseball player

PANTHRS 2 COYOTS 2

Dan the man
Former vice president and creative speller Dan Quayle is among the many non–sports celebrities who have been honored in ESPN highlights.

dishes to Ham / Who goes to the basket for the one-handed slam.") There has even been an occasional political highlight. Former vice president Dan Quayle showed up at an NHL game so dull that his presence was, for once, almost newsworthy. In Quayle's honor, all proper names in the highlight were misspelled, and the final score was posted "Panthrs 2, Coyots 2."

But in highlights, as in sports, there can be no meaningful creativity without a solid grasp of the fundamentals. If you can't dribble, you sure as hell can't dribble between your legs. And the simple, straightforward Who Won? highlight is as fundamental as the dribble, but much harder to execute. You can't understand just how hard without paying a visit to ESPN's screening room.

The screening room is a vision of purgatory. It's not even a room, really—it's more of a pit that lies in the basement of ESPN headquarters, a warren of brick buildings surrounded by satellite dishes. Upstairs, in the building's public sector, carpeted hallways are lined with autographed jerseys of famous athletes, preserved under glass like giant insect specimens. Even farther upstairs, executives sit behind desks as big as hog farms, and autographed balls perch like chubby little kings on little glass thrones. It is *good* to be an ESPN executive.

But down in the screening room, it is not so good. There's just one desk, a small one, shared by two harried highlight supervisors ("Hi Supes" in the jargon of the place). The room itself is one huge horseshoe-shaped shelf heaped with video equipment, computers and dozens of flickering screens. Each screen is tuned to some live sporting event, with a production assistant—a sleep-and-food-deprived young person, generally no more than a year or two out of college—hunched in front of it, typing or scribbling preposterous minutiae, such as: "1:11:43 Pierzynski fouls pitch off foot"; or "2:08:37 Jeter in on-deck circle, takes practice swings w/metal bat, grimaces." This is called "logging," which simply means taking note of every damn thing that happens. There are no autographed uniforms in the screening room; the only decoration is a handwritten sign taped above the door, reading: "LOG LIKE A CHAMPION TODAY."

The noise is ungodly—dozens of sportscasters blather from dozens of television sets, crowds roar, telephones jingle, questions are shouted and ignored, then re-shouted and answered by five impatient voices at once. It's a little like a stock exchange, except no one in the screening room is making any money to speak of. They are making highlights instead.

"I couldn't last five minutes buried in that room," says *SportsCenter* anchor Steve Levy. "It's dark and it's cold and it's loud—I don't know how those kids focus on their games. If they go to the bathroom, and miss some unbelievable play, the whole country might miss it, too. Often a kid is writing [the game details] as the highlight is still being edited and someone upstairs [in the studio] is screaming for the tape. And if it's not perfect—if Carlos *Beltran* gets a hit and the kid writes Carlos *Lee* instead, and Dan Patrick reads it on the air. . . " Levy pauses, and looks a little ill; then, just perceptibly, he shudders. "Oh, I wouldn't want to deal with it. Would not want to deal with it."

Well, John Farmer is willing to deal with it. He is one of about 140 production assistants at ESPN, hired from a pool of thousands of applicants. Why he was selected, he is not exactly sure. "We hire PAs for a million different reasons," explains Bill Graff, senior coordinating producer. "Some are book smart, some are sports nuts." As far as he knows, Farmer has never been described as "book smart." Whatever. The point is, he has seven months to prove to his bosses that he deserves a permanent job. About 75 percent of PAs make it; the rest are let go.

On the first Saturday of the college football season, Farmer takes a seat in the screening room between two TVs, for he has been ordered to monitor two games simultaneously: Michigan vs. Central Michigan, which is expected to be lopsided target practice for Michigan QB John Navarre; and the much more evenly matched Wisconsin vs. West Virginia, which pits the Badgers' thoroughbred running back, Anthony Davis, against the Mountaineers' slick QB, Rasheed Marshall.

Farmer cannot pretend to be a neutral observer. "My grandfather actually died at a West Virginia game," he says. "Heart attack. The ultimate highlight, I guess." As the Mountaineers rush onto their home field, his own heart seems to clutch in his throat just a bit. Smiling cheerleaders, deliciously fit and pretty, lead the way in a sprint, dwarfed by the hulking, double-wide players, jogging behind in their home blues. From out of nowhere, the Mountaineer mascot, who looks exactly like a young Daniel Boone, leaps into the tableau and the thunderous cheering practically lifts Mountaineer Field into the air. "Killer stuff," whispers Farmer:

So young, so lost In the bowels of the beast—ESPN's Bristol, Connecticut, screening room—production assistants subsist on a nourishing diet of sports, junk food and sports.

"He wants Texas back."
—Tommy Lasorda, Dodger manager, on Fernando Valenzuela's contract demands

Most Memorable
Anthem Renditions

■ There's more of an aura around pre-game national anthems than ever before. There's anticipation about who's going to sing the anthem on Opening Day, at the Super Bowl, before the Indy 500. All the time, the video is rolling, and anthems have become news events and entertainment spectacles in and of themselves. Which is why, even if we weren't there in person, even if they weren't broadcast live, we've all had the chance to see the best—and the worst.

1. Roseanne Barr, San Diego Padres home game, June 25, 1990
Roseanne's screeching delivery before a Padres-Reds doubleheader, followed by obscene gestures, was so bad it merited comment by President George Bush, who called it "a disgrace."

2. Marvin Gaye, 1983 NBA All-Star Game, February 13, 1983
His soulful, funky, 2:35 rendition had the crowd at the Forum in Inglewood clapping and swaying. VH1 included it as one of the "100 Greatest Rock & Roll Moments on TV."

3. Natalie Gilbert and Maurice Cheeks, NBA playoffs, April 25, 2003
Natalie Gilbert, 13, forgot the lyrics before an NBA playoff game between Portland and Dallas. As she noticeably struggled, Portland coach Maurice Cheeks spontaneously left the bench area to give the girl an assist. He put his arm around her shoulders, and together they sang a duet that moved and inspired the crowd of 20,000 at the Rose Garden.

The perfect stage-setting footage for his highlight.

Early in the first quarter, Wisconsin's Alex Lewis blocks a West Virginia punt that bounces into the Mountaineers' end zone, where the Badgers recover. Two middle-aged Wisconsin coaches suddenly feel young again and celebrate like homeboys. They leap into the air and try to slap palms, but one, who looks a little like Ted Baxter, elevates no more than two centimeters, leaving his colleague swiping at the air. It's a wonderful moment of unselfconscious exhilaration, and Farmer chuckles delightedly. Perfect comic relief for his highlight.

Then the tape deck breaks.

Farmer remains calm as a worried-looking technician arrives and stuffs his hand rudely down the machine's mouth. With little confidence in this sort of repair work, Farmer prowls the room for an empty video recorder. These are not plentiful on the first Saturday of college football, but he finds one, just as Rasheed Marshall is rolling to his right and looking downfield. Poor Marshall doesn't see the Badgers' Lewis streaking towards him until—kah-BLANG!—Lewis explodes into Marshall's belly, laying him out on the turf like a dead man. Farmer clucks his tongue sympathetically, but he's also tapping his foot with excitement: a perfect scene-stealer for his highlight. The game is still close, but in the second half, Mountaineers' tailback Quincy Wilson goes down clutching his knee. Farmer clucks his tongue again—a perfect follow-up to the Marshall hit.

All the while, every minute or so, Farmer's eyes shoot over to the Michigan–Central Michigan game. He breathes a sigh of relief as Michigan runs up the score, 45-7. All he'll need to do for that highlight is pluck out Michigan's best offensive plays, and that should pretty much tell the story of the blowout.

Back in West Virginia, Anthony Davis has decided not to let Wisconsin lose, breaking loose for a total of 167 yards. As Davis motors into the end zone for the winning touchdown, Farmer honors his grandfather, muttering, "I hate the Badgers." But this will be a sweet, sweet Who Won? highlight. Farmer looks a little like Anthony Davis himself as he trots to an editing studio with videotapes from both games under his arm. There, with editor Joe Frady spinning knobs furiously, the Wisconsin victory plays out again: The Mountaineers take the field, the punt is blocked, the coaches celebrate like doofuses, Lewis disembowels Marshall, Wilson goes down, and Davis runs away with the game. Farmer carefully annotates each key play for the anchor (whoever he or she may be—he has no idea) on a rough script or "shot sheet." He notes each situation ("first quarter, no score"), each event ("punt blocked") and each result ("coaches celebrate like doofuses"). This is all the anchors get. "We give 'em the meat and potatoes," says Farmer, "and they throw in the herbs—all the 'booyahs' and stuff."

It takes 90 minutes to edit both games and supervisors keep running in and out to kibitz and hurry him along. (After one supervisor kibitzes for the second time in 10 minutes, Frady waits for him to leave, and then does his best Bogart imitation: "Of all the gin mills and editing rooms in this crazy world, he had to walk into mine.") But when Farmer emerges, he's smiling like a champion. Each story is told with admirable brevity: the Wisconsin–West Virginia highlight is two minutes long; Michigan–Western Michigan, a minute and change.

Unfortunately, Jon Lavoie, a young supervisor with a broad football body and a "we-can-do-it-if-we-buckle-down" attitude, has bad news for Farmer. He puts a hand on the kid's shoulder like a coach about to tell a player that, in spite of all his hard work, he's going to be benched. *SportsCenter* has scheduled just 50 seconds for the Wisconsin–West Virginia highlight. In other words, it'll have to be cut by more than half.

There's a deer-in-the-headlights look on Farmer's face that highlight manager Paul Dunn has seen thousands of times in his 18 years at ESPN. Like a game warden, Dunn watches out for PAs caught in the crosshairs and leaps to their rescue. Looking at Farmer's tape, he's impressed. "Hold on to this," he says, removing it from the video recorder, for it is a perfect Who Won? highlight and could be a good résumé-booster. Nonetheless, Dunn doesn't sugarcoat what Farmer needs to do next: That opening tableau, with the cheerleaders and the mascot? It's out. The hilarious celebrating coaches? Out. Quincy Wilson's injury? Out. And by the way, both highlights have to be reedited in less than 45 minutes.

It's 5:15. Farmer has eaten nothing since breakfast except a Jolly Rancher lollipop (and he won't, until after 10). But he fastens his chin strap—or would, if he had one—and dives back into the editing room for the second half, so to speak.

This is what it takes to make a great Who Won? highlight: all the same qualities it takes to be a great athlete, except for muscles, foot speed, agility and all of that other athletic stuff—the warrior spirit, indefatigability, practice and teamwork. And if there was any justice in the world, the

4. **Meat Loaf, MLB All-Star Game, July 12, 1994**
His moving rendition in front of 59,568 fans at Three Rivers Stadium was widely praised.

5. **Grover Washington, Jr.'s tenor sax renditions for the Philadelphia 76ers**
In the early 1980s, Washington, who recorded a song titled "Let It Flow (For Dr. J)," was both a good luck charm for the Sixers and one of the best national anthem players of all time.

6. **Whitney Houston, Super Bowl XXV, January 27, 1991**
With the first Gulf War looming, she belted out a rendition that sold 750,000 copies in eight days. She was lip-synching.

7. **Carl Lewis, New Jersey Nets home game, January 21, 1993**
The great track star ripped off a terrible rendition before a sellout crowd of 20,049 at the Brendan Byrne Arena, there to watch the Bulls play the Nets. His voice cracked while singing "rocket's red glare," after which he ad-libbed "uh-oh" into the lyrics, then paused before the final verse to tell fans "I'll make up for it now." He didn't, mangling the final verse.

8. **Bleeding Gums Murphy**
In the second season of *The Simpsons*, the "Dancin' Homer" episode, Springfield resident jazz musician Bleeding Gums Murphy played a rendition before a Springfield Isotopes baseball game. It lasted 26 minutes, according to the stadium clock.

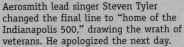

9. **Aerosmith, Indianapolis 500, May 27, 2001**
Aerosmith lead singer Steven Tyler changed the final line to "home of the Indianapolis 500," drawing the wrath of veterans. He apologized the next day.

10. **Smokey Robinson, World Series Game 5, October 23, 1986**
His rendition at Fenway Park was one of the best ever.

UNIFORMS TO DIE FOR

■ You'll notice something odd about this list—all of the worst unis have been fashioned in the past 25 years. Meanwhile, the best unis are a mix of both the new and the old. What's up with that? For one, there's something about timeless classics that we dig. And the bad? It's only been recently that designers have had such a wide array of disgusting colors and fabrics.

1. New York Yankees

2. Oakland Raiders

3. L.A. Lakers

4. Baltimore/Indianapolis Colts

5. L.A. Dodgers

6. St. Louis Cardinals

7. Detroit Red Wings

8. St. Louis Rams

9. Portland Trail Blazers

10. Penn State Nittany Lions

UNIFORMS THAT DESERVE TO DIE

San Diego Padres

2. Pittsburgh Pirates

3. Marshall University

Mid-1970s Indians

5. 1981 White Sox

6. 1982 White Sox

7. 1979-80 San Diego Clippers

Orlando Rage (XFL)

9. Houston Rockets

10. New York Mets

"We were given a **choice**. We could **either** run around the field **three** times or run around Tommy Lasorda **once**."

—Steve Sax, former Dodgers second baseman

Who Won? highlight would be enough to satisfy any audience.

But it is not enough, because after a while, all those Who Wons start to look the same. And ESPN's search for alternatives would ultimately revolutionize not only sports broadcasting, but sports itself.

One of the first signs of ESPN's simmering revolution occurred in 1985, though few recognized it. The Phillies trounced the Mets by a score of 26-7 and, that night, to the horror of Mets fans and the delight of New York–haters, ESPN's highlight showed 16 of the 26 Philadelphia runs crossing the plate, one after another, bang-bang-bang-bang-bang-bang-bang-bang-bang-bang-bang-bang-bang-bang-bang-bang. This sort of video collage is common today. You might see it when Kobe hits 10

shots in a row, or when Martin Brodeur makes 40 saves in a row or when Quincy Carter throws 15 incompletions in a row. But it was an eye-popping innovation at the time.

The same year saw the debut of *NFL Gameday*, hosted by Bob Ley, Tom Mees and Jack Youngblood. It was the latest sally in the network's ongoing assault on pro football. The program aired on Sunday mornings and, though its highlights were no great shakes at first, fans appreciated the fact that it played no favorites. The other networks often pretended that the games they just happened to be airing were, coincidentally, the most important of the day—a conceit that bred distrust in many a viewer. *Gameday* (later renamed *NFL Countdown*), on the other hand, always put what it considered the best game first and always told you why it was best.

The program's potential was so obvious, even the NFL brass saw it, and, in 1987, the league made an unprecedented deal with ESPN. "We got the rights to show highlights from every game, and to use them however we wanted," says Bob Rauscher, now senior coordinating producer of ESPN's NFL studio shows.

Berman hosted, and Sunday invariably brought out the best in him. Like a kid let loose in a Toys "Я" Us, he'd explode with enthusiasm over each new thing that caught his eye. Even today, his off-camera body language betrays his boyish excitement. His eyes pop as he watches the action on his monitor, his legs wriggle, he pokes Tom Jackson and waves his arms wildly, urging a punt returner into the end zone as he booms: "HE COULD . . . (wave) . . . GO . . . (wave, wave) . . . ALL . . . THE . . . (wavewavewave) . . . WAYYYYYYYYY!"

"That's when we started to show some non-chronological highlights," says Rauscher. "All kinds of possibilities opened up

"Son, looks to me like you're spending too much time on one subject."
—Texas A&M basketball coach to a player who got four Fs and one D

to us: We could show all 12 plays in a great 12-play drive. We could focus on a matchup between a receiver and a defensive back. We could look at an offensive sequence, then look at the same sequence from the defense's point of view. Of course, it took a while for all these approaches to develop."

Indeed it did, for the various forces struggling for control of the network were still divided about where to take it. "CNN's *Sports Tonight* was actually beating us," recalls Ley with indignation. In truth, there was no great shame in that, as the Atlanta-based CNN was then the undisputed champ of 24-hour news. It delivered a broad sweep of sports, under the more-than-capable stewardship of Bill MacPhail, a former president of CBS sports. "He seemed to have a personal relationship with everyone in sports," marvels Rick Davis, who produced *Sports Tonight.* And the fact that CNN's owner, Ted Turner, had a financial interest in both the Braves and the Hawks—"well, that didn't hurt either," chuckles Davis.

Déjà vu all over again In June of '85, an ESPN highlight showed 16 Phillies scoring against the Mets, one after another, in quick succession. The technique—commonplace today—caused quite a stir, especially in New York.

> "The **real tragedy** was that **15** hadn't been **colored** yet."
> —Florida head coach Steve Spurrier, on a fire at Auburn's football dorm that destroyed 20 books

All chuckles aside, "CNN was the originator in terms of sports news coverage," writes Keith Olbermann, who joined the network in 1981, despite a distinct lack of TV experience. (When he left for WCVB-TV in Boston in 1984, he would be replaced by none other than his future *SportsCenter* partner, Dan Patrick.) But the network made a fatal mistake when it decided to concentrate less on highlights and more on analysis. Its groundbreaking investigative program, *A Closer Look*, paved the way for both ESPN's *Outside the Lines* and HBO's *Real Sports*. But Olbermann and Davis (now head of Standards and Practices for CNN) feel that a corporate decision to emphasize financial news at the expense of sports fatally crippled CNN's effort to compete with ESPN.

There were other competitors, too, not to be taken lightly. George Michael has never gotten the credit he deserves for

launching his *Sports Machine* on Washington, D.C.'s WRC-TV. Like Rasmussen, Michael saw the future in 1979, and convinced his bosses to invest $800,000 in a satellite hookup to snare whatever national highlights they could. On Sunday nights, he would stand in front of a high-tech backdrop that looked like a set from *Spaceballs* ("I designed it myself," he says proudly), rolling nothing but highlights for a whole half hour. "People just could not believe how many highlights we had," he says today, "and soon, all the NBC affiliates wanted to air us." He remains popular to this day, because he exudes a plainspokenness that ESPN has deliberately eschewed, sometimes to its detriment. "Let me ask you something," he says, "which ESPN anchor would you want as your local sportscaster? Which one? I'll tell you: none of 'em!"

Man and machine George Michael sensed the national appetite for highlights even before ESPN did, and his syndicated Sports Machine program remains popular even after two decades on the air.

In many ways, Fred Roggin of KNBC, Los Angeles, was ESPN's most creative competitor and, certainly, its most iconoclastic. Roggin started from a subversive premise: "Sports shows are like tonic waters. They're all made from the same stuff, so they all taste pretty much the same. What makes Canada Dry different from Schweppes? The packaging! We decided to look for new ways of packaging sports stories—so entertaining that even people who didn't like sports could enjoy 'em."

Roggin specialized in what he called "mini-movies"— little storyettes with cartoon sound effects and weird voiceovers. He was so original and outlandish that by 1990 his legendary *Roggin's Heroes* program was nationally syndicated. There was parody ("Mr. Roggin's Neighborhood"), blooper reels ("The

Hall of Shame") and kooky characters, like Officer Feldman, a poker-faced security guard who stood behind Roggin all through the broadcast and never said a word.

Roggin was enormously controversial, even at his own station. Once, he recalls, at a KNBC retirement party for a respected executive producer, he shook hands with the retiree and asked him why he'd decided to call it quits.

"I'm retiring," the producer said icily, "because of assholes like you."

Roggin watched ESPN carefully, with increasing unease as the years went by. He understood the network's potential at least as well as anyone in Bristol. "I remember thinking, 'Wow! They've got so many resources, they could become nearly impossible to compete with.'"

Shooting star *When ESPN executive editor John Walsh decided that the day's best moment should lead each* SportsCenter, *a young man from Chicago started showing up almost every night.*

Barry Sacks, who produced the 11:30 *SportsCenter* in the 1980s, is an Everyfan, a rumpled, beer-barrel-chested guy with a permanent five o'clock shadow. His look of self-satisfaction could be mistaken for smugness, but it's nothing of the kind. Sacks is just a guy who couldn't be happier about the way his life has turned out, his every waking hour a festival of sports. He speaks rapidly, as people who always feel a deadline looming learn to do. "*Nobody* wanted to work at the show," he says. "It meant working 'til three in the morning and getting very little credit. We'd run all these chronological highlights and then put up the final scores. One thing we did do, beginning, I think, in '87, was start to take the Rotisserie approach. Everyone was in fantasy leagues by then, so we started putting up more and more individual stats. But we were still a scores-and-highlight machine. Until Walsh appeared and transformed us into a news organization."

"Walsh appeared"—generally, that is how people put it when they speak of ESPN executive editor John Walsh, for his appearance is rather arresting. He's an albino (that is, his skin, hair and eyes are as white as chalk) and looks rather like Dumbledore, the head wizard at Harry Potter's Hogwarts School. Indeed, words like "wizard" and "visionary" are often used around ESPN to describe Walsh—though, it must be added, other words like "overrated" and "needs to be stopped" are also some-

■ In the 1960s, hair went wild. It took a while (and free agency, and the highlights culture) for athletes to catch on, but since ESPN took to the airwaves, we've seen some outrageous personal hair statements. So we present the good, the bad, the weird, and the just plain ugly.

■ Carlos Valderrama   ■ Dennis Rodman   ■ Pat Riley

■ Brian Bosworth   ■ John Daly   ■ Jaromir Jagr

■ Marv Albert   ■ Dennis Rodman   ■ Venus Williams   ■ Scot Pollard

■ Dwayne Schintzius   ■ Jerry Rice   ■ Andre Agassi   ■ Gene Keady

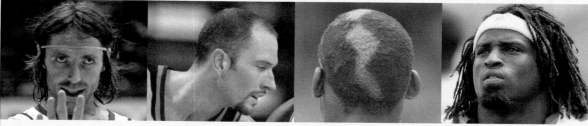
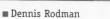

■ Steve Nash   ■ Rex Chapman   ■ Dennis Rodman   ■ Ricky Williams

HAIRDO'S AND DON'TS

■ Tony Kornheiser

■ Ken Dorsey

■ Lou Henson

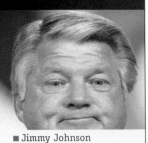

■ Jimmy Johnson

■ Ben Wallace

■ Wesley Stokes

■ Carl English

■ Dan Dickau

■ Quin Snyder

■ Tonya Harding

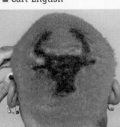

■ Dennis Rodman

■ Françoise Mbango Etone

■ Ronaldo

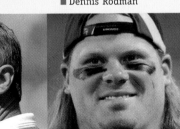

■ Jim Tressel

■ Chris Hovan

■ Darius Songaila

■ Latrell Sprewell

■ Kevin Greene

■ Keith Closs

■ Dennis Rodman

81

"The terrible thing about my job is that players get 80 percent of my earnings."
—Sports agent Eric Hall

times used, albeit a little more cautiously. Precisely how much credit Walsh deserves for *SportsCenter*'s transformation is hotly debated by network veterans, but there's no denying that the revolution occurred on his watch.

Walsh was hired in 1988 and was controversial from the start. A former editor at *Rolling Stone, Newsday*, and the *Washington Post,* and co-creator of *Inside Sports* magazine, he was far better known for his ink-and-paper work than for the smattering of TV he'd done. (He's equally famous for what is thought to be the most extraordinary Rolodex in journalism, containing private numbers for not only athletes, but movie stars, fashion models, politicians and, quite possibly, you.) "I got the job in January," he says, "and I didn't even go down to the newsroom until June. I stayed up on the third floor, watched all the shows and developed various theories."

One theory was that if ESPN really wanted to "establish *SportsCenter* as a show of record . . . with hard, Page 1 sports news," it wouldn't be done by putting the kibosh on Berman's nicknames, or otherwise stifling the program's admirable sense of humor. Instead, Walsh reorganized it like a newspaper. "Up 'til then," remembers Steve Vecchione, then a young *SportsCenter* producer, "it went like this: 'Here are the American League highlights,' then we'd go to break. Then we'd come back and it was: 'Here are the basketball highlights,' then we'd take a break." Now a Bulls victory that ended with a hoop by Michael Jordan might lead the show; but this might be followed by a story on Mike Tyson's latest kerfuffle; which, in turn, might be followed by a hockey game that had to be repeatedly stopped because of all the seafood hurled onto the ice by fans. More important, says Sacks, "in highlights, the question became less about who won than *why* they'd won." Was the story Greg Maddux? The Braves' defense? Or the mascot, Chief Nokahoma? "Whatever it was, we started trying to tell that story in as entertaining and creative a manner as we could. And because it was a story, we wouldn't tell you the result until the end. I mean, who tells a story by starting at the end?"

Not everyone appreciated all of these changes. Walsh says he faced "normal resistance" in his first few years, but that just makes Ley laugh. "I used to drive him home a lot," says Ley, for Walsh is legally blind and cannot drive himself. "He used to talk to the dashboard about how hard a time he was having. He'd talk about change and order-

out-of-chaos. But he wouldn't tell me; he'd tell the dashboard."

One of Walsh's most controversial changes involved meetings. "Believe it or not, there were very few editorial meetings before he came," says Ley. "So he started having them, to talk about ideas. He'd announce them with a bell, and that *was* weird—this half-blind albino guy ringing a bell. People would come in mooing like cows."

But it was at one of these meetings, in April of 1990, that the breakthrough occurred. The third Monday of that month is Patriot's Day in Boston, a celebration of the city's role in the American Revolution. Two sporting events are traditionally held: a Red Sox Game at Fenway Park, beginning at 11 A.M., and the Boston Marathon, which commences in the town of Hopkinton an hour later. In Walsh's afternoon meeting, it was reported that Patriot's Day of 1990 had been a nightmare, even for Red Sox fans accustomed to humiliating defeats. Boston had been slaughtered by the Milwaukee Brewers, 18-zip. In fact, someone noted with a snort, the ballgame itself had been a marathon: Even though the game had started first, the winner of the race had crossed the finish line before the last out was recorded.

"You could tell John had an idea," remembers Steve Vecchione. You could almost see a lightbulb go on over his white, furry head.

Rites of spring The Boston highlight was a montage that included mesmerizing herds of runners, Dave Parker's fearsome stick, and Italian marathoner Gelindo Bordin's victory.

"David Cone is in a class by **himself** with three or four **other** players."
—Yankees owner George Steinbrenner

Here's to the winners The sweet swings of Robin Yount and Gary Sheffield, the third Boston Marathon victory for Portugal's Rosa Mota—it doesn't get any better.

"I was going to write myself in, but I was afraid I'd get shot."
—Raiders tackle Lincoln Kennedy, explaining why he didn't vote

"Let's put them together," he suggested. "Show both events at once, with a timeline." Vecchione was a Walsh fan, but this idea struck him as nearly impossible. "There was so much *tape*," he remembers—about five hours' worth. And it would be excruciating to get the timeline right, matching the key moments from the game with the key moments of the race. The show was understaffed, the chance of success was small—

"Try to look past all of that," said Walsh. A silence descended on the room.

"It was a hard sell," says Walsh.

"I'm sure it was," says Ley. "For years, people had been afraid of being thrown out of an airplane if they failed."

It wasn't until Walsh said the magic words—"if it doesn't work, it's *okay*"—that the staff snapped into action. Vecchione handed the job to Chris Lincoln, one of his best production assistants. And one of ESPN's rising stars, a Mr. Dan Patrick, wrote and narrated it. The highlight is a revelation even today.

It opens with a spectacular panoramic shot of Boston—Fenway Park, a rich green ruby in the foreground under a silver sky, with the smooth Boston Bay glistening to the east. "Looks can certainly be deceiving for New Englanders," Patrick begins. "It appeared to be a picturesque day in Boston. Thirty-five thousand packed Fenway park, while a million lined the streets of Boston for the marathon." At 11:08, the Sox's Mike Boddicker is seen delivering the first pitch at Fenway and the umpire calls an enthusiastic strike. Meanwhile, Bud Collins, one of Boston's odder sportscasting institutions, is shown in a dizzying houndstooth jacket, pink shirt and red bow tie, "loosening up for the marathon coverage." Then the Brewers, in their pajama-like uniforms, begin sending cannon shots crunching into Fenway's Green Monster, and three runs cross the plate. The scene then switches over to Hopkinton, where 8,000 marathoners take off like one huge slow-rising animal. "Milwaukee kept running as well," says Patrick, as Edgar Diaz is seen plating Dave Parker and Greg Brock for a 6-0 score. At the same time, marathoner Juma Ikangaa breaks away from the pack with a small group of elite runners. Ikangaa, a diminutive Tanzanian, is clearly the crowd favorite, but Boston crowds will not be getting their way today.

Fourteen minutes later, the Brew crew struck again," continues Patrick, "as Parker doubled in B.J. Surhoff to bury Boston, seven to nothing. At the same time, Rosa Mota surfaced as the women's leader in the marathon." On it goes, Brewers tearing around the Fenway bases, marathoners pounding the Boston streets. Just as it starts to become relentless, the Brewers' Dave Parker leaves the game and Boston fans spontaneously leap to their feet and cheer him with all their might. Parker, nearing the end of his brilliant career, is obviously moved and a bit surprised, and tips his cap with emotion.

"The game between Ikangaa and Italy's Gelindo Bordin was just beginning," continues Patrick, as both run on exhausted, slurping water from plastic bottles. Then, at 1:46, the Brewers' Greg Vaughn "hits the wall"—that is, he makes a spectacular catch against the Monster. "At the same time," says Patrick, "so did Ikangaa"—and the Tanzanian is shown completely whipped, trudging up the marathon's notorious Heartbreak Hill. Sports history was made everywhere: Bordin would be the first man to win both an Olympic gold medal and a Boston Marathon. Mota became the first woman to win the event three times. And the Brewers completed the highest scoring shutout in team history.

The highlight leaves you with a strange sensation, something beyond sports. It's as if you, yourself, have spent a dizzying spring day in Boston, a day you have no wish to forget.

"It's my favorite highlight of all time," says Bill Graff. "It was the talk of the place." Vecchione received a congratulatory letter from company president Steve Bornstein. And Walsh? "I was *ecstatic!* This was *just* the direction I wanted us to go." ∎

"**What we have is a highlights slide.**"
—L.A. Kings PA announcer David Courtney, on why he wasn't preparing a highlights video of the previous season

CHAPTER 5

Highlights Take Over the World

ESPN'S NEW DIRECTION WAS ACTUALLY MANY DIFFERENT directions at once; in fact, as many as possible. Dan Steir, then highlight coordinator, began circulating a list of 17 different kinds of highlights throughout the company. "Of course, there are more than 17, many more, an infinite number," he says today. "The idea was just to help people start thinking about the possibilities." Nonetheless, the list has become a classic of sorts and still pops up sometimes at ESPN training seminars. The trick is not only to become familiar with all the tried-and-true possibilities it suggests—the Turning Point highlight, the Key Series highlight, the Key Matchup highlight, and so on—but also to understand which approach is most appropriate for telling the story of a given game.

Take, for instance, the Cutaway highlight. This technique is most useful when the actual game is of little interest. One of the most memorable cutaways ever concocted arose from a dreadful display of basketball between St. Joseph's and the University of Rhode Island.

The highlight commences with a closeup of St. Joseph's mascot, the St. Joe's Hawk, and a voiceover explains that, according to tradition, he must flap his wings ceaselessly throughout each game, from opening tip to final buzzer. Then attention turns to the game: "The play on the court was awful chippy," the voiceover says. Just how chippy? URI's center is

---

And the Lord says, you got to rise up! Master of the Hero highlight, Michael Jordan lifted ESPN and other sports companies to new heights.

"A lot of good ballgames on tomorrow, but we're going to be right here with the Cubs and the Mets."

—Thom Brennaman, Chicago Cubs broadcaster

shown holding the ball in the lane, looking as if he's trying to remember something completely unrelated to basketball, like the chemical symbol for cadmium or William McKinley's running mate. Then, as if suddenly realizing where he is, the poor guy tries to put up a shot, but it's blocked before it even leaves his hands. St. Joe's grabs the loose ball and races wildly downcourt. A guard sets up behind the arc and starts to take a jumper, but from the corner of his eye, he sees a URI defender charging toward him and panics in mid-jump. Unable to commit to any definite course of action (*Pass? Shoot? Hold?*), he compromises and tosses the ball more or less straight up over his head. Believe it or not, it's only afterward that, as the voiceover says, "things get ugly . . . between the mascots!" The Rhode Island Ram (a student in an oversized goat costume) tries to prevent the St. Joe's Hawk from flapping his wings, and is chased onto the court by the enraged bird, who literally loses his head. Surreally, the human head of a wholesome-looking but incensed St. Joe's student sits atop the bird's neck, frantically waving his wings, stomping his talons and hellbent on kicking the Ram's ass. A referee restrains the Hawk before any blood is shed, while the ram, looking remarkably like Eddie Haskell, watches with delight. "The Hawk flaps undaunted," concludes the voiceover with mock drama, as St. Joe's coaches lead their nearly apoplectic mascot away. "But Rhode Island wins, ninety four to seventy six."

Not only is this cutaway highlight much more fun to watch than any Who Won? could have been, it better conveys the sloppy-but-passionately-fought tenor of the game. And so, with a green light from Walsh, *SportsCenter*'s Barry Sacks began teaching his PAs a new equation: More Creative = Better.

"What I've always loved about this place," says Sacks today, "is that ninety-nine percent of our most important editorial decisions are made by young, entry-level people." From the beginning of his mentoring career, he urged his young people to fall in love with this fact, too, and to relish their unique position as gatekeepers of America's sports consciousness. "Don't just transcribe the *game*," he would say, "transcribe your *emotions*. If you say 'Wow!,' Joe Blow from Iowa is probably gonna say 'Wow!,' too. Imagine that you're the only person watching the game, because, in a very real sense, you are. If something great happens and you don't bring it to us, nobody sees it, and if nobody sees it, it's as if it never happened. Everything great must make our highlights—somehow.

The Seminal Seventeen

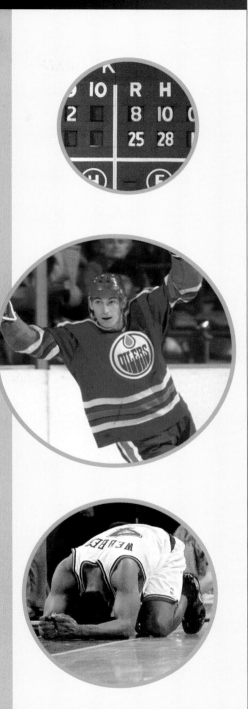

■ ESPN's Highlight Revolution began in earnest in the early 1990s, when producer Dan Steir sat down to make a list of all the different ways the story of an athletic event could be packaged. The list was far from complete, but that was the point: "There are an *infinite* number of ways to tell these stories," says Steir. But to this day, a good 90 percent of highlights seen on ESPN fall into one of these categories:

1. The "Who Won?" Highlight

Also known as the "Chronological" or "Old Fashioned" highlight, it's the least ambitious way of reporting a sporting event. The big plays and key scores are revisited in the same order in which they went up on the scoreboard.

2. The Epic Highlight

Every good storyteller, from Homer to George Lucas, knows that the beginning is not always the best place to begin the telling. This highlight picks up the action at some thrilling juncture in the middle, then teases the audience with backstory and buildup—before revealing the final climactic result.

3. The "Hail, Conquering Hero!" Highlight

Sometimes a great, charismatic player, like The Great One himself, just won't let his or her team lose. The story of such a game is often best told focusing primarily on that player's heroics.

4. The Blowout Highlight

Nothing is more boring to a sports fan than a blowout. On the other hand, nothing is more excruciating for a loser, and here, no effort is made to preserve the losers' dignity. Instead, the audience goes on a Dante-esque tour of sports hell, revealing all the most grotesque, hideous details of a humiliating loss—score after score after score by the winner, failure after failure by the loser. It's cruel, but it's fun.

5. The "Just Put a Gun to His Head and Put Him Out of His Misery" Highlight

Sometimes the outcome of a game comes down to one player—a kicker, a goalie, or a shooter like Chris Webber—and, sometimes it just ain't that player's day. The spotlight is trained on this unfortunate "*goat*" and his or her failure is mercilessly dissected.

6. The "Put a Gun to ALL of Their Heads and Put Them ALL Out of Their Misery" Highlight

Like the above, but the collective errors of a team are reviewed.

7. The Defense Wins Highlight

Low-scoring games can appear dull—until the intricate complexity and ferocious tenacity that a winning defense requires are probed and revealed.

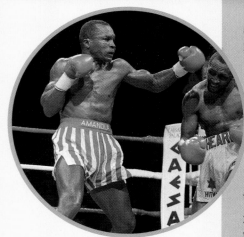

8. The Offense Rules Highlight

High-scoring games are, of course, thrilling—and here is captured the near-absurdity of the roller-coaster emotions that accompany such a contest.

9. The Clash of the Titans Highlight

The Big Matchup is one of the grandest spectacles in sports—Bird vs. Magic, Montana vs. Marino, Roger vs. Pedro, or Sugar Ray Leonard vs. Thomas "Hit Man" Hearns. Here, the game becomes little more than a backdrop to that spectacle.

10. The Turning Point Highlight

Sometimes the outcome of a contest turns on a single event, and this highlight shows the hows and whys.

11. The Single Series Highlight

While not a "*turning point*" as such, a series of events may dramatically illustrate why a game was won or lost. For instance, a long, relentless offensive drive may seem to leave a defense impotent and deflated for the rest of the day.

12. The Blue Collar Highlight

Innumerable games are won because of superior "dirty work"—great picks, great blocks, great throws to the cutoff man—that no one notices. This highlight *makes* them notice.

13. The Cutaway Highlight

What do you do when a game is just plain boring or bad? Cut away! Focus on fans or mascots, or something in between like Hogettes, and watch them watch the action. The results can be hilarious.

14. The "Do You See a Trend Here?" Highlight

Sometimes a highlight can show the story of a contest in a particular strength of the winner, or a weakness in the loser. Perhaps ground balls hit to the left side kept finding their way through the infield, or a hockey team's defense kept the crease clean as a whistle, all night, with check after check.

15. The Game Plan Highlight

Did one team or another have a brilliant, or controversial, pregame strategy? Did it work? The answer probably had much to do with the final score.

16. The Controversy Highlight

A game may hinge on a questionable call, as it did on the notorious Tom Brady "tuck rule" play in 2002, when officials denied the Raiders a fumble recovery. Highlights can be used to analyze such plays six ways from Sunday—or even Doomsday.

17. The History Highlight

Was a record broken, or a milestone passed? Haul out the memories, let the teardrops fall, and mark this special event with highlights, old and new.

And that's where the creativity comes in: *How?*"

Fifteen years later, Sacks can still sometimes be heard giving this speech to new PAs—just as enthusiastically as the first time he gave it—and it always makes Mike McQuade smile. Now a senior coordinating producer, McQuade came of age as a PA under Sacks and fondly remembers the shift, as he puts it, from "just telling the story" to "the sense that you had to do something different. I did my first creative-type highlight in, I think, 1990. The Pacers creamed the Jazz and we went down the roster, showing each Pacer, one by one, as he scored. When I got to Greg Dreiling, I had to stop, because he just refused to score. But that was my first, and ever since, I've been involved in trying to find new ways to tell these stories."

It may seem like little more than a gimmick. But it's a good deal more than that. "It's storytelling," says Neal Pilson, a former head of CBS Sports who now oversees an elite sports-marketing firm. "And it was storytelling that turned out to be the true genius of *SportsCenter*—not the shouting or the sarcasm or the smartass attitude. Each highlight became a mini-story about an event. You didn't know the outcome of the vignette, or even what you were going to see, until the highlight was over. That's just great storytelling, and that is how ESPN turned the highlight into an art form."

Sportswriter Mike Lupica has named our era "the highlight generation." Almost all of our sports, he writes, are now "geared to quick bursts" that can be digested by TV viewers instantaneously, if not quicker. Significantly, the highlight generation began in earnest right around 1990, while Mike McQuade was learning his craft and waiting, in vain, for Greg Dreiling to score.

Off with his head! *The fall of Eastern European communism was a boon to the NBA and other sports-related Western businesses.*

The early '90s were, of course, a climactic time in world history: The Cold War ended, the Internet revolution erupted, the first worldwide fiber-optic network was completed . . . and Michael Jordan won his first championship.

Granted, some of these events were more crucial to the march of human progress than others. But the simultaneous maturation of Michael Jordan and ESPN's highlight-making elves would actually help launch one of the great cultural sea changes of the 1990s. "It was quite a decade," writes Cornell

Jackson of all trades No single sport, let alone a single team, was a big enough stage for Bo. Fortuitously, his career commenced in 1986, just as sports marketing began to shift dramatically from teams to individual stars.

"All I said was that the trades were stupid and dumb, and they took that and blew it all out of proportion."

—Twins pitcher Ron Davis, reacting to press coverage of his comments criticizing front-office maneuvers

University historian Walter LaFeber in his classic study *Michael Jordan and the New Global Capitalism*. "An era made possible by Jordan's athletic skills, his marketing instincts, a new type of corporation exemplified by Nike, and the technology of communication satellites and cable that made the globe into one mammoth television audience." In other words, for better or worse, Jordan and ESPN, with a little help from their corporate friends, would turn the world into a global sports village.

ESPN's highlights were already transforming the emphasis of American sports coverage from local to national. "Remember, before ESPN, almost all of the highlights you saw revolved around local teams and local athletes," says Pilson. If you lived in Boston, you saw Celtics highlights; if you lived in Detroit, you saw Pistons highlights; and that meant that "if you didn't live in L.A., you wouldn't see a highlight of Jerry West more than once every few months." So even the hottest sports celebrities—those invited to appear on Wheaties boxes, or in shaving cream commercials where Farrah Fawcett crooned, "Let Nox-eee-ma cah-*ream* your face . . . so the razor *don't!*"—even those lucky jocks rarely had the cachet of, say, an A-list movie star or a top-drawer pop singer. An athlete just couldn't get the same kind of relentless exposure.

But then up jumped ESPN, collecting highlights from hither and yon, packaging them with ever-increasing skill, and launching them into living rooms, coast to coast, *every night*. If the Royals' Bo Jackson made an impossible throw to the plate to nail Mariners speedster Harold Reynolds, you didn't have to live in Missouri or Washington to see it. Under Walsh's "may the best story win" policy, you'd very likely see it leading off *SportsCenter*, whether you lived in Altoona, Pennsylvania, or Angels Camp, California. What's more—this was key—you'd see them do battle the following night, too. Or take future Hall of Famer Phil Niekro: Over five years, he would move from the Braves to the Yankees to the Indians to the Blue Jays and back to the Braves again. But wherever he went, there he was, tossing butterflies past mighty sluggers—because *SportsCenter* followed him from uniform to uniform. All of which meant that if an athlete was skilled enough, and charismatic enough, and got enough nighttime lovin' from ESPN's highlight reels, there was no reason why he, or she, couldn't be as big a celebrity as anyone in America! Sure enough, '80s jocks began showing up on TV commercials with a frequency that was actually quite annoying, until you got used to it: "Tastes great! . . . Less filling! . . . I must be in the *front row*!" It was obviously the start of something big.

Of course, ESPN was not *solely* responsible for this nationalization of sports. But in the final analysis, "it was ESPN that opened the door for national sports celebrities," says Pilson. Not only because of its 24-hour dedication, but also because of the artistry in its highlights. As the '80s ran their course, and the network's reach grew from 7 million households to 54 million, ESPN's highlight makers perfected the most influential, and controversial, of highlight genres: the Hero highlight.

The Hero highlight, of course, declares one player a lion among pussycats and lays before him a lion's share of praise. It bestows upon him bountiful kudos; it gives him mad, mad props; it bows down before him and cries, "We are not worthy!" Once upon a time, coaches—and especially basketball coaches—*hated* Hero highlights, because heroes are individuals, and teams, not individuals, win games. But, according to historian LaFeber, three irresistible forces came together to overrule coaches in this regard, and made the Hero highlight the very essence of modern sports marketing.

The first irresistible force was the NBA itself. As hard as it may be to believe now, 20 years ago, the league was neither popular, nor a money machine. When the Chicago Bulls reluctantly drafted Michael Jordan in 1984 ("There wasn't a center available," lamented Bulls general manager Rod Thorn. "What can you do?") the franchise was reckoned to be worth less than $19 million. Clearly, the league needed a new business plan, and commissioner David Stern came up with a doozy. He would run it like an entertainment conglomerate. In fact, he would run it very much like Disney, the company that now owns ESPN. Why Disney? Well, he later explained, "they have theme parks, and we have theme parks . . . [though] we call

> **"He should have been better, pitching on 3,195 days' rest."**
> —Pirates broadcaster Steve Blass on Jimmy Boudreau, a strike replacement player. Boudreau hadn't pitched for nine years.

Following Phil *In the mid-1980s, Phil Niekro changed teams four times in four seasons, but a 24-hour sports channel allowed a nation of knuckleball fans to watch their hero pitch himself into the Hall of Fame.*

93

"**Nobody's ever lost** four **straight** big ones—unless **you count** the French"
—Tony Kornheiser on the Bills' four straight Super Bowl losses

It's a world of hoops (opposite)
Michael Jordan made so much money for American companies, at home and as far away as Beijing, that Nike president Phil Knight would call him "the greatest endorser of the 20th century."

them arenas. They have characters: Mickey and Goofy. Our characters are named Magic and Michael."

Now who could argue with that? Well, almost anyone with enough dignity to resent being compared to Goofy. On the other hand, as commissioner, Stern probably had reasons for expressing himself as he did. The point, as Pulitzer Prize–winning journalist David Halberstam put it in *his* Jordan study, *Playing for Keeps: Michael Jordan and the World He Made*, was that "individual players were now being promoted [by the league] rather than teams."

The second irresistible force was Nike, whose sales had doubled between 1987 and 1989 to $1.7 billion. The company revolutionized the athletic footwear industry, chiefly by hiring Wieden + Kennedy to come up with one of the most successful marketing plans in history. "Nike understood that people don't buy shoes based on rational benefits," explained Ty Montague, Wieden + Kennedy's co-creative director. "Eighty percent of all basketball shoes never touch a basketball court. People buy basketball shoes because of the badge value of wearing them, the way it makes them feel to wear a certain brand."

But how do you invest a pair of, um, sneakers, with "badge value"? Simple, said Montague: You "give consumers a compelling and entertaining story" based on "humor and interest and engagement and not being annoying." More specifically, you show videos of the Ultimate Athlete, enacting *the ultimate sports highlight*—while wearing Nike sneakers!

Just in time, Nike's chief competitor, Reebok, launched a purely "rational" ad campaign, bragging that its shoes were made of only the finest materials and designed with extraordinary care. Wieden + Kennedy was delighted. "Reebok brought a knife to a gun fight," Montague would later crow. The Nike campaign would be pure fantasy: Wear Nikes, and you can soar like a jetliner; wear Nikes and your potential will be limited only by your imagination; wear Nikes and you could one day team with Bugs Bunny to *save the world!* All of these ideas would be transmitted in what were, essentially, 60-second highlight reels. All that was needed was that Perfect Athlete to star in them.

Which brings us to a third irresistible force, Michael Jordan.

There was little for ESPN to brag about in its early coverage of His Airness. During Jordan's first game at North Carolina in 1981 (he was referred to as "Mike Jordan" throughout the

■ Over these past 25 years, we've seen an explosion in the number of sports fans. Fans have become part of the event, part of the story. And they've also become highlight staples as they've become more creative in showing their passions. The signs and banners have gotten more creative, the ways to cheer and jeer have multiplied, and some painted faces are almost works of art. But for our list we looked to the diehards—the folks who went to games year in, year out, fair weather or foul. And to groups of fans that, well, we (and the opposing teams) could never forget.

1.The Dawg Pound

In 1985, Cleveland Browns cornerbacks Hanford Dixon and Frank Minnifield started calling their defensive linemen "dogs" as a motivational technique. When the line made a particularly good play, Dixon and Minnifield would bark at them. And the fans loved it, especially those sitting in a 10,000-seat section behind the end zone in the old Cleveland Municipal Stadium. Browns players came to the Pound before every home game to get psyched up, and the opponents—warming up nearby—could be hugely intimidated by the fan force.

The Dawg Pound mercilessly taunted opponents, and threw dog biscuits. And they were loud, so loud that the opposition couldn't hear anything but the Pound noise.

The Dawg Pound lives on, thanks to the "new" Browns and the new Cleveland Browns Stadium, which has built into its design a close replica of the old Pound.

"There was nothing as organized as the Dawg Pound," said former Browns nosetackle Bob Golic. "A community formed in those stands that transcended everything else. Bankers, attorneys, guys who pumped gas stood there, arm-in-arm, barking until they were hoarse. It was a thing of beauty."

2. Harry Grossman

On August 8, 1988, Grossman, 91, turned on the lights for the first night game at Wrigley Field. Why Grossman? Because by that time he'd seen about 4,000 Cubs games at Wrigley, going further back than 1907, the year the Cubs

became the Cubs. "I'm here, rain or shine, hot or cold," he said back in '88. "I came when there were five hundred, a thousand people here. I figure, if they can play, I can watch." Grossman died less than three years later.

3. Elizabeth Dooley

Dooley attended more than 4,000 consecutive games at Fenway Park,

starting during WWII, and not missing a contest until a year before she died in 2000. "She's the greatest Red Sox fan there'll ever be," said Ted Williams. "She was just a perfect lady," said Dom DiMaggio. "I remember so well when she presented us with our American League championship rings after we won in 1946. She was so thrilled. The Red Sox were practically her whole life, from what I could gather." The day Dooley died, the Red Sox lost to the Yankees, 22-1.

4. Raider Nation and the "Black Hole"

Raider Nation might exist within a geographic area whose unmarked boundaries are somewhere in the Bay Area. Or Raider Nation might be a mindset—a state of frenzied loyalty to the silver and black of the Oakland Raiders. Silver and black are key: You want to be part of Raider Nation, you wear the colors, and, if you've got some swagger, a costume with horns won't hurt. Tailgating is okay, too: Some citizens of Raider Nation set up shop in the Network Associates Coliseum parking lot days before home games. The party is long and hard, continuing through the game and after. Be prepared for action, too—some say Raiders fans are the rowdiest in the NFL.

The "Black Hole" is a famous Raiders fan group that began in section 105 of the Coliseum when the Raiders returned home to Oakland. First there were seven friends, passionate fans all. Then 20. Now the numbers are countless, the tailgating incredible, and the hole has expanded to include two sections on either side of 105.

Be prepared to wear the colors. And to stand for the whole game.

5. Jack Nicholson

Lakers players come and go, but one thing you can count on seeing every time you tune into an L.A. home game is Jack's mug. He's got fabulous courtside seats and is an impassioned rooter. In 1980, he got into a fight with Bullets coach Dick Motta. Jack told *SI's* Rick Reilly the story in 1986: "He was up screaming and out of his box and I was standing in his way and he said, 'Hey, sit down!' And I said, 'You sit down!' He said, 'This is my job, man!' "And I said, 'I pay money for these seats!' Then he went out on the court, and I followed him out there. I told him it would take somebody bigger than him to sit me down— or something really intelligent like

that. Ever since, he's been scared to death. He don't even coach 'em in the Forum. He just sits in his little seat and never gets up."

Nicholson's such an impassioned fan that he has season tickets to the Clippers, just so he has good seats when the two L.A. teams face off. He used to travel to away games regularly—he famously mooned a Boston crowd one time—but has curtailed his hoops travel. Still, after 25 years or so, he'll do just about anything to avoid missing a home game.

"You gotta remember my line of work," he explained. "Sports is the only place I can go and not know how it's going to end."

6. John Adams

Back in Cleveland Municipal Stadium, fans could make a lot of noise by beating on the old chairs. When those chairs were removed in the early 1970s, Adams, an Indians fan, missed the percussive beat. So he asked the Indians if he could bring a drum to the games.

Since August 24, 1973—for 30 years—Adams, his wife (who introduced herself at a 1974 game) and his bass drum (for which he buys a ticket) have been to all but 18 Indians home games (day games, when he had to work), making lots of noise in the right field bleachers. Adams became a big-screen icon with the release of *Major League* in 1989—the fans beating the drums in that movie are based on Adams and the occasional sidekicks who join him.

Adams is beloved by Indians players, management and fellow Indians fans, and was recently feted on his 30th anniversary as the Indians' greatest fan. He's spent all of his adulthood—since he was 21— beating that drum, and he still has no plans to stop.

7. Robin Ficker

Ficker's been called a heckling genius, and is widely hailed as the most erudite (and effective) fan there's ever been, at least when it comes to hurling abuse at opponents. Ficker, a trial lawyer and Bullets fan, was, for 12 years, a fixture behind the Washington Bullets/Wizards bench. His modus operandi: Do anything to break the opponents' concentration, but the following rules apply— nothing racial or sexual, no swearing, no drinking, and no booing. Ficker's genius also included plenty of sweat—lots of research on opponents to find their psychological weak spots, and lots of time putting

together costumes and props.

Once, Vernon Maxwell got into a brawl at a restaurant, and Ficker got under his skin by dressing as a waitress. Another time, he distracted the Bulls by reading specially selected passages from Phil Jackson's autobiograhy. He used another Bulls appearance to do a reading from *The Jordan Rules.*

Best of all, his shtick worked— Jordan got so angry he threw a basketball at Ficker. Jackson completely lost it. And Charles Barkley dumped a bucket of popcorn on his head.

When the Wizards moved to their new arena in 1997, they wouldn't give him his customary seat behind the opponents' bench, so Ficker retired from the pros and focused on college basketball.

8. Texas A&M's "12th Man"

A&M's original 12th man was basketball player E. King Gill, who

during the January 2, 1922, game against Centre College, when the Aggies were short on reserves, was called down from the press box and asked to suit up, in case he was needed. A&M won, 22-14, and Gill never played. Which he regretted. "I wish I could say that I went in and ran for the winning touchdown, but I did not," he said. "I simply stood by in case my team needed me."

The 12th man is now the entire A&M student body, which stands throughout every Aggie home game—ready to leap out of the stands and onto the field in case their team needs them. Regular students even try out to be an on-field 12th man, a representative of all the students who actually plays on A&M's kickoff team.

"We all get **heavier** as we get older because there's a lot **more** information in our heads. Our heads **weigh** more."

—Vlade Divac

broadcast), analyst Bucky Waters remarked to ESPN's Jim Simpson that "people are comparing [Jordan] to Walter Davis and David Thompson. He really *is* a good player." A few years later, when it became clear that he was a little bit better than that, Jordan gave ESPN's Roy Firestone a major scoop, saying "without equivocation" that he would not leave college early to turn pro. A few weeks later, Jordan entered the NBA draft.

By 1990, Jordan was certainly soaring, but he did not yet rule. Larry Bird had dubbed him "God disguised as Michael Jordan." Director Spike Lee had filmed Nike's "Michael and Mars Blackmon" commercials, popularizing the memorable slogan: "It's gotta be the shoes." This campaign proved so successful that Jordan was now collecting $17 million a year in endorsement money from various clients. Combined with the relatively paltry $3.25 million he received from the Bulls, his annual income was now greater than the team's net worth in his rookie year. But most important, he was not simply the most popular *athlete* in the United States. According to polls, he was tied with Bill Cosby for the title of most popular *celebrity*. It *could* be done! "Owners and sponsors no longer saw themselves competing against rival teams or even rival sports," wrote David Halberstam. "Now they were competing in a far larger and more cutthroat arena—against rock stars, movies and all kinds of other forms of modern entertainment—for a slice of the entertainment dollar."

But there was still one knock on Michael in 1990: He'd never won a title. It had to hurt when Hall of Fame coach John Wooden, the closest thing to a conscience basketball had left, gently refused to rank him among the game's elite. "He's a show within himself," Wooden said, "not a team player."

Jordan was a man of many implausible contradictions, and one was that he was about to find a way to be a team player while remaining "a show within himself." As he chewed up the league that season, Hero highlights featuring Michael were called for just about every time the Bulls played. The traditional formula for such highlights was well established: They would begin with a shot of the hero stretching his hammies or playing H-O-R-S-E with his teammates before the game. Then they would perfunctorily summarize the first half, showing swishing baskets at both ends (you had to do that, even if the game was a blowout, just to provide some drama). Then, the voiceover would rise and say something like: "In the third, MJ took charge!" There would follow a few "Wow!" shots of Our Hero swishing and slamming, the final score would be posted, and there was your highlight.

Well, that wasn't enough for ESPN anymore, nor did it do justice to Michael. His Hero highlights had to reflect the excitement of seeing him, of never knowing what he would do next. And some of the most effective Hero highlights ever created at ESPN put it to you just like that: "What will Michael Jordan do?"

Maybe the voiceover asks this question as MJ sets up behind the arc, guarded by Thunder Dan Majerle or some other All-Star, windmilling his arms and shifting his feet. The picture freezes, and it's multiple choice: Will Michael (a) shoot? (b) drive? or (c) pass? Nothing so simple: He'll fake the shot, juke Thunder Dan, streak into the lane, stick out his tongue at the "help defense" (which, like the cops, always arrives too late), and then—the screen freezes again. "What will Michael Jordan do now?" His patented One-Handed Pipe Dunk? The ferocious Two-Handed Cram, which practically unravels the net? Or will it be Rock the Cradle, deftly moving the ball from left to right, while in midair, before pounding it through the trembling rim?

Sales Spike *Nike and Lee used Jordan's highlight appeal to turn the lowly "sneaker market" into an international juggernaut worth billions.*

Nothing so crass: On this occasion, it pleases him to kiss the ball home with a dainty layup. Then he winks, knowing what everyone had expected, and that he'd fooled 'em.

Nothing like it had ever been seen before, not in the NBA, not anywhere in the world. Luckily for the world, everything was going global: basketball, ESPN and satellite-delivered commercials featuring Jordan. Nike President Phil Knight watched his sales explode—to $9 billion by 1997—and called Jordan "the greatest endorser of the twentieth century." Historians like LaFeber agreed: The three American-based companies best known around the world were Nike, Coke and McDonald's—"and it is no coincidence that Michael Jordan endorsed them all." By 1993, the only global celebrity who rivaled him was Princess Diana.

But for ESPN, the lingering moral was this: "Sports marketing today is focused almost entirely on individual athletes," says Pilson. "And that is because of highlights." ∎

"Some quiet guys are inwardly outgoing."
—Ralph Kiner

CHAPTER 6

Mr. Dictionary Gets a Makeover

THE HIGHLIGHT-FUELED ELEVATION OF SPORTS CELEBRITIES was so lucrative—and *SportsCenter*'s role in it so crucial—that the marketing of *SportsCenter* itself soon became focused on individuals, too. ESPN's anchors grew increasingly famous, and they deserved to be, for every new innovation and wrinkle concocted by the production department made their already tough jobs a good deal tougher.

Live television is always unforgiving, but sports television, with its infinite minutiae of stats, trivia and rules, offers unique challenges. These challenges are known, variously, as sports geeks, sports nerds and sports junkies. There are millions of them out there, they all watch *SportsCenter* and they all take sports very, very seriously. If Roger Clemens throws a splitter, and you mistakenly call it a forkball on the air, every last one of them will dial up directory assistance in Bristol, Connecticut, to find your home number so that they can explain the difference to you. As a *SportsCenter* anchor, you have no margin for error. You are not allowed to stumble over a name like Przybilla, nor mispronounce one like ZhiZhi, nor are you entitled to snicker just because a NASCAR driver's name happens to be Dick Trickle, or a Florida State receiver is named Craphonso Thorpe. By snickering, you risk implying that you may not have heard of Trickle or Thorpe until seeing their names on your TelePrompTer, and that is an implication

Teammates of talk By mastering the sport of shtick, Keith Olbermann and Dan Patrick turned SportsCenter *into a cultural phenomenon.*

"If I weren't earning $3 million a year to dunk a basketball, most people on the street would run in the other direction if they saw me coming."

—Charles Barkley

no ESPN anchor can bear. For the anchors are themselves a collection of the most inveterate sports geeks, sports nerds and sports junkies in the world.

It is touching how much pride they take in their own geekitude. For instance, ask the ESPN anchors to name the most remarkable sports highlight in history, and few will mention the Immaculate Reception, or the Shot Heard Round the World, or anything of that nature. More likely, they will tear up a bit and mumble something about Super Bowl XXI, in 1987, when quarterback Phil Simms led the New York Giants to a 39–20 victory over John Elway's Denver Broncos at the Rose Bowl. Simms got the MVP award, but in the annals of anchors, the greatest performance of the day belonged to Chris Berman.

The game had just ended and Berman was waiting to narrate his postgame highlights. As always at a Super Bowl, fleets of satellite trucks had been set up by television networks from across the nation and beyond the seas, with rivers of television wires snaking throughout the Rose Bowl grounds—one of which connected to Berman's monitor. But just moments before Berman was supposed to go on the air, someone unplugged that very wire.

Who could have *done* such a thing? Certainly no one from another network, for that would have been ungentlemanly, unladylike and unsporting. True, ESPN had signed a groundbreaking deal with the NFL earlier in the year, and certain fellas at certain networks were rumored to be plenty steamed about it. But nothing was ever proved, so history will simply note that Chris Berman had no way of seeing the Super Bowl highlights he was about to narrate for a nationwide audience.

And yet Berman never broke a sweat. A frantic producer began hissing into his earphone a rough description of each play as it appeared on screen (e.g., "Okay, now Simms is gonna throw it to Bavaro, I think"). Berman effortlessly retrieved each play from his memory bank, dusted it off (mentally speaking), and calmly described it as though it were unspooling before him. No one would ever have guessed that he was flying blind. That is why he gets to be on television and millions of sports geeks who think they could do his job have to stay at home and watch him.

But such emergencies are rather rare. The nightly challenge of *SportsCenter* is simply to make highlights—which, despite all the creativity that goes into them, are bound by their nature to be repetitive—seem a little bit different each time. And no one ever met this challenge with more enthusiasm, and ferocity, than Keith Olbermann and Dan Patrick.

Olbermann joined the network in 1992, yielding, like a bashful maiden, to more than four years of courting by the persistent Walsh. Alas, their quarrels would later become legendary (Olbermann would bewail that Walsh once berated him in "vile, unceasing, condescending and inappropriate language"). But not before he was assigned to the 11 P.M. *SportsCenter* with Patrick. Suddenly, TVs across America lit up with newly minted catchphrases.

Olbermann and Patrick were determined to replace the hoary clichés of yesteryear with a snazzy lexicon of new ones. (A catchphrase is, by definition, a cliché that has yet to wear out its welcome.) Patrick had grown tired of saying that hot-shooting or hot-hitting or hot-however players were "on fire"—a phrase he'd lifted from Marv Albert, who had doubtless lifted it from somewhere else. A cameraman suggested to Patrick that he might try saying, "*el fuego*," which was Spanish for the same thing—except that it wasn't, quite. A Spanish teacher soon wrote in to point out that "*el fuego*" means "*the* fire" rather than "*on* fire," and that the phrase Patrick really wanted was *en fuego*.

Why the use of a couple of Spanish words so delighted millions of viewers is a pickle, especially since many of them apparently had no idea what Patrick was saying. San Diego Chargers running back Natrone Means once asked Patrick to say "that thing you say . . . the one that begins with 'n' . . . n fuego!" But on blacktops and playing fields across the United States, kids started squealing it whenever they were pleased with themselves, and they are still squealing it to this day.

The rest of Patrick's best-loved catchphrases seemed to favor the monosyllable: In hoops, a made shot was just plain "Goot!" In baseball, a home run was simply "Gawn," and a strikeout was "Thahhh . . . whiff." Olbermann was wordier. In hockey, you scored by "puttin' the biscuit in the basket"; a disappointed team was said to be "drooling the drool of regret into the pillow of remorse." Even when he was at a loss for words, Olbermann was never at a loss for words, for he might resort to: "I have nothing more to say about that that is either relevant or true" or "Mr. Dictionary has failed us yet again," as Mr. Dictionary is bound to do when you require so much of him. When the pair finally sat down to write a book, *The Big Show*,

Mighty mouths Like Laurel & Hardy or George & Gracie, Olbermann & Patrick were widely imitated, but never equalled.

En fuego! Goot!

. . . puttin' the biscuit in the basket

"He's missing something upstairs, but that's what makes him a player."
—Tony Phillips of the California Angels on teammate Rex Hudler

MOST STYLISH ATHLETES

■ What athletes wear—and how they wear it—caught our attention more than ever before. Some superstars are among the best-dressed celebs in the world. Many have become walking advertisements for different fashion lines. And, in the past quarter century, sports has played a huge role in creating fashion trends, in everything from shoes to urban wear to jewelry to the now ubiquitous retro jerseys.

■ James Blake   ■ Serena Williams   ■ Scottie Pippen

■ Kristi Yamaguchi   ■ Tiki Barber

■ Dave Winfield   ■ Dominique Dawes   ■ Evander Holyfield

■ Michael Jordan   ■ Anna Kournikova   ■ Tiger Woods

> **"He's going to be out of action the rest of his career."**
> —Mets broadcaster Ralph Kiner on Braves reliever Bruce Sutter's injury

about their experiences on *SportsCenter*, they counted some 76 catchphrases "more or less regularly in use"—which really meant that they had graduated from catchphrase to full-blown shtick. Best of all, it was shtick that vividly expressed the network's point of view, as previously stated herein: reverence for sports, irreverence for the conventions that surround it.

And so ESPN began to market Olbermann, Patrick and the rest of its *SportsCenter* "talent" (the TV business word for "announcer"). Weiden + Kennedy produced a long-running series of hilarious "This Is *SportsCenter*" skits. Stuart Scott and Kenny Mayne would try to teach Kobe Bryant and Keyshawn Johnson how to say, "I'm the *man!*"; Olympian Dan O'Brien would hold out his javelin so Dan Patrick could hang his ties on it and choose the prettiest one; Linda Cohn dropped off her kid at a day care center run by Evander Holyfield; and so on.

The conceit behind all of these giggly commercials was based on a surprisingly serious issue: the delicate balance of power that exists between *SportsCenter* and the athletes it covers. Everything in an athlete's life can be made, or unmade, by the highlight machine—from salary and endorsement opportunities to the equally important gossip that circulates among their parents and spouses.

For the anchors, every one of them a wide-eyed sports fan

***Head over heels** Highlights of Super Bowl XXVII showed the Buffalo Bills might have made a game of it, if only they had changed their cleats.*

at heart, maintaining that balance can be a heady experience. Imagine finding yourself in the presence of your own sports heroes, icons known the world over for their strength and skill, and to have them acknowledge, however jocularly, that *you* wield a certain power over *them*.

"After being at ESPN for a while, you find that players sort of seek you out, when you come into the locker room, or whatever," says Steve Levy. "It gives you your own little taste of celebrity. And I think they assume that if they go out of their way for us, we'll cut 'em a break when they need it."

Memo to players: Don't count on it. "There are hundreds of players, and there are millions of viewers," says Levy. "So my first responsibility will always be to the viewers."

In August 2003, Oakland Raiders veteran linebacker Bill Romanowski—his skills disintegrating, but his personality still as pungent as ever—threw a temper tantrum in practice and socked tight end Marcus Williams in the eye, putting his teammate out for the season. Even for Romanowski, who had been previously fined for spitting in the face of receiver J. J. Stokes, breaking QB Kerry Collins's jaw and walloping tight end Tony Gonzalez in the head, it was an amazingly asinine move. But what was far more amazing to the editorial staff of ESPN was this: Since practices aren't filmed, there was no video of the tussle. It seemed almost metaphysically impossible: How could something of consequence be said to have "happened" in the sports world if no highlight existed? "It was shocking," said Levy. "Sure, I could *tell* the story, but . . . it's not the same. Believe me, that is rare. Rare, rare, rare."

We of the Highlight Generation are the luckiest sports nuts ever. Fans have always hated one sensation more than any other, and that is the sensation of having missed something. That, too, has become rare, rare, rare. Not only do we see "everything great," as Sacks puts it, but we see it better than ever before. No strategy is too arcane to be deconstructed and dissected by experts, and no subtlety too well hidden to escape notice.

A particularly memorable example: Dallas' 52-17 humiliation of Buffalo in Super Bowl XXVII. After the slaughter, Joe Theismann narrated a distressingly convincing highlight that showed the Bills might have improved their chances immeasurably simply by changing their cleats. "All through the first half, all you saw was cleats being changed on the Cowboy side," he pointed out, while the Bills made no adjustments for

Best Owners

■ What makes for a great owner? The No. 1 criteria is a desire to win. No. 2 is loyalty—to the hometown, to the fans, to the players. No. 3 is good old success.

■ Packers fans around the world

In 1922, Green Bay sold shares of its football club, and the Packers remain (and will, under current NFL rules) the only team in football to be publicly owned. About 1,900 fans, at last count, from every state and several foreign countries, own shares of Packers stock, which is, in a sense, worthless. It can't be sold, it can only be passed down to family or sold back to the Packers. The shares don't increase in value—a $25 share bought in 1950 is still worth $25 today. The team is nonprofit, meaning if it's ever sold for hundreds of millions, profits will go to build a war memorial in Green Bay. So, ownership is about one thing, pure and simple: loyalty. When the team needs to raise extra cash, it can sell more shares with the permission of the NFL. Fans line up for a chance to "invest" in their team's future.

■ Wellington Mara (New York Giants)

Tim Mara, his father, bought the Giants in 1925, and Wellington, then nine, saw the first game the team ever played. When Wellington assumed control in 1965, six years after his father's death, the Giants saw many good years and many lean ones. They won Super Bowls with good people. And had terrible seasons. But throughout, Mara has been a mensch—patient, graceful, compassionate and generous. "I know of no owner since I've been in the NFL that equals Well's contributions, his fairness, his decency," said Ravens owner Art Modell in 1997. And few would disagree.

continued on page 109

United colors of basketball At the 2002
*World Basketball Championships, the
highlight-minded ballhogs of Team USA*
(opposite) *were outclassed by the teamwork of
Yugoslavia* (above)*, Spain and Argentina.
Many sportswriters blamed "the ESPN factor."*

the sloppy field conditions. Then Theismann showed a replay
of Bills tight end Pete Metzelaars skidding into the turf as a
pass meant for him sailed into the arms of a sure-footed
Cowboy defender. "Pete Metzelaars did not have the right kind
of cleats on his feet," Theismann scolded. "We saw Bruce
Smith slip, we saw Thurman Thomas slip, we saw Kenneth
Davis slip . . ." And sure enough, there they went, splat, splat,
splat in the replays, as Theismann concluded disgustedly:
"Everything turned out to be . . . one . . . big . . . slip!" To
paraphrase Ben Franklin, for want of a cleat, a season was lost.

And for want of a highlight, that moral, too, would have
been lost. Look how much good a highlight can do in the world:
It shows us an aspect of the game we were likely to have missed;
contributes to the overall quality of sport by demonstrating to
coaches and players (or at least, those on the Buffalo Bills) how
to improve in the future; and teaches us, and our kids, a valuable little lesson about life: Don't forget to change your cleats.

So highlights are what Martha Stewart would call "a good
thing" . . . are they not? The fan is always the first priority,
but athletes love 'em, too—"more validation for us," says former baseball star Brian Downing—and, as we have seen,
they've made the business of sports more profitable than
Albert Spalding could ever have dreamed. But as Martha

Stewart's many detractors like to point out, there are times when you can get too much of a good thing. And the 25th anniversary of ESPN is just the time to reflect on how, sometimes, highlights can hurt.

The game of basketball is now said to be suffering the effects of a highlights-borne illness. The only question is whether it's an annoying, skin-deep condition like hives, or something more dire.

This illness has been a long time germinating. George Michael got his first whiff of it more than 20 years ago at a high school game in Maryland, just a few years after he'd cranked up the *Sports Machine*. Two of the region's powerhouses were at war: Baltimore's Dunbar and Hyattsville's DeMatha Catholic, coached by Hall of Famer Morgan Wooten, who would retire in '02 with a jaw-dropping record of 1,274–192. "In those days, DeMatha had a star named Adrian Branch," Michael remembers, a player who radiated with NBA potential. "And I'll never forget it: He came flying down the court on a breakaway, threw the ball off the backboard, caught it himself, and dunked it himself." Of course, everyone in the building went nuts—except Coach Wooten. Branch's play contradicted everything Wooten had ever tried to teach about teamwork, sportsmanship and fundamental basketball. He was livid, and not just with Branch. "I appreciate your being here, George Michael," he barked. "But the reason he did that was to make *your highlights*."

"Well," some may say, "so what? Branch's play, like so many hoops highlights, may not have been great basketball, but it was fabulous television. And since the idea of television (and, to a large degree, spectator sports) is to entertain, why not just sit back and enjoy it when an exuberant player shows off a little bit? Are coaches so dedicated to winning that they're allergic to a little fun?"

continued from page 107

Jerry Buss (L.A. Lakers)

Buss, a real-estate tycoon, bought the Lakers and the Forum in 1979, and with that he brought showtime—razzle-dazzle entertainment for the rich, the famous and the masses. "I really tried to create a Laker image, a distinct identity," Buss said. "I think we've been successful. I mean, the Lakers are pretty damn Hollywood." His formula—fast-break basketball, cheaper cheap seats and more expensive courtside seats, and, most important of all, a focus on the fans, led to a surge in attendance, a couple of Lakers dynasties and eight NBA championships.

Mark Cuban (Mavericks)

Is there a single player in the NBA who wouldn't want to play for Mark Cuban? The ultimate fan-as-owner, Cuban doesn't merely mingle with the common folk at Reunion Arena, he sits among them, as he did before he was owner. And he screams and yells so much he racks up tremendous fines. Cuban doesn't only publish his e-mail address, he responds to messages from everyone, at all times. Finally: He made the Mavs into winners, spending big bucks to take the team to its first playoff appearance in 11 years in his first year as owner, 2000-01.

George Steinbrenner (Yankees)

There's a lot to like about George, and a lot not to like. But the bottom line is he wants the Yankees to win, and he'll do whatever he can to do it. His methods are sometimes questionable, but his motives are clear. If we had a "worst owners" list, he'd make that, too.

continued on page 110

continued from page 109

■ Jack Kent Cooke (Redskins)

Cooke became majority owner of the Redskins in 1974 and took over day-to-day operations in 1980. In 1981, he hired San Diego offensive coordinator Joe Gibbs as head coach. Two years later, the Redskins won the Super Bowl. In 1988, they won again, and again in 1992. In the 1990s, he built a great new training facility, and then got a great new stadium built despite tremendous obstacles. In short, Cooke took a so-so franchise and made it into a great one; one that bound together the Washington, D.C., area (and, along the way, became the most valuable franchise in the NFL). And he did it with great style.

■ Ted Turner (Braves)

Turner, who bought 100 percent of the Braves in 1976, was brilliant, using his once-little TV station (WTBS) to promote the Braves. When he made money off his cable enterprises, he invested plenty of it in the Braves, and then used Braves games as a centerpiece of the WTBS "Superstation" lineup. It was a long-term, build-a-dynasty strategy that worked. The Braves became one of the most popular baseball teams in the country because of the national exposure. And then they went from being a laughingstock to one of the greatest teams ever, making the playoffs year after year after year.

■ Miles Wolff (Durham Bulls)

In 1980, he spent a few grand to bring baseball back to Durham, North Carolina. Wolff did practically everything himself in the early 1980s, promoting the Bulls' great old ballpark and building the best attendance in Single-A ball, despite a terrible location in the city. He and the Bulls deserve much of the credit for reinvigorating minor league baseball. The Bulls inspired a great baseball flick, and eventually raised Durham—new stadium and all—up to AAA level.

A lot of people *used* to say stuff like that, but they've been an awful lot quieter since the fall of 2002, when basketball's highlight disease became a bona fide crisis. It blew up in Indianapolis, when USA basketball sent its Dream Team to the World Championships. Most of the league's top stars chose not to attend, but no matter; failure was not even a concept, let alone an option. The U.S. team was still loaded with NBA All-Stars; how could it lose to countries that boasted no more than a few NBA players per team?

By superior teamwork and fundamental basketball, that's how. The Americans played as if defense was an inconvenience and passing an indignity; as a result, our fellas were embarrassed by Argentina, Yugoslavia and Spain—three countries, by the way, whose *combined* population is less than one third of ours. Indeed, the spirited, floor-savvy, ball-sharing squads from abroad were such an appealing contrast to Team USA that many American fans found it hard to root for their own country. The nadir of the tournament occurred when a frustrated Jermaine O'Neal, looking like a playground bully, stomped on the back of an Argentine player while he lay helpless on the floor.

How did it come to this? Every sportswriter in the land seemed to know. Barry Jackson of the *Miami Herald* called it "the *SportsCenter* factor. Young [American] players, eager to be showcased on ESPN or other highlights shows, are more concerned with making the spectacular dunk or behind-the-back dribble than learning back cuts or free-throw technique." Jim Litke of the Associated Press was even more blunt: "That's what you get," he scoffed, "from players who stand around on defense for a season's worth of NBA games watching middling talents trying all night to make one highlight-reel move."

Is it possible that highlights, with their emphasis on individual showmanship, are ruining basketball?

"Oh, sure," deadpans Bob Ley. "And, by the way, we caused the Enron scandal, too."

"Aw, *of course not*," groans Bill Walton, as he searches for a Waltonesque metaphor to express just how much the idea appalls him. "That's like . . . like blaming rock 'n' roll for the decline of Western civilization. It's just the opposite. Just as Bob Dylan, Jerry Garcia and Bruce Springsteen *improved* life as we know it, ESPN improves basketball. Basketball is an extremely visual and personal experience, and, to me, the best parts of it are the mental and emotional aspects. Television captures those emotions and allows everyone to enjoy the rewards of being involved in the game. ESPN has expanded the experience, not diminished it. I mean . . . come on."

He's mostly right; but he's a little bit wrong, too. For all of the exhilaration and happiness it brings, rock 'n' roll can also make you deaf if you aren't mindful of the volume. And that's what seems to have happened to basketball highlights—the volume has gotten a little too loud.

"I believe that the highlights *have* hurt basketball," says John Wooden in a sagely voice more suited to a philosopher than a warrior chief who led his Bruins to 10 NCAA championships between 1964 and 1975. "When a perfect give-and-go gets a smattering of applause and a fancy but meaningless dunk gets a roar, that's got to influence a young player. That's got to undermine the team game. I always coached the *unspectacular* in basketball, not the spectacular—what happens away from the ball, both offensively and defensively. That doesn't show up in the highlights; but it *does* determine whether you win or lose."

The problem, of course, is that unspectacular basketball makes for unspectacular television. "That's why we feature the reverse 360 slam dunk," says Levy. "In fact, you might see the same dunk up to six times in a one-hour show—in the tease, in the bumps, in the Top Ten plays of the night. You gotta sell stars, and a star is somebody who stands out from the team."

Wooden is not the only one to note the negative effect of all of this on young players. "We've always had crazy characters in the NBA," Charles Barkley declared on ESPN, with a perfectly straight face. "The difference now is . . . these guys don't want to be great players. They want to be on *SportsCenter* and make all that money." Magic Johnson, sitting next to Barkley, vigorously nodded his agreement. Elsewhere, revered coaches from John Thompson to Spain's Javier Imbroda have said much the same. Indeed, Imbroda, who led the Spanish national team over the U.S. in Indianapolis, claimed that the skills of his best player, Pau Gasol, had actually been *corroded* by his Rookie-of-the-Year season in the NBA. "Selfish game," he huffed. "Always a player, not the team."

But wait, it gets worse. An increasing number of very smart

■ Peter Magowan (SF Giants)

In 1992, it looked like the Giants would be moving to St. Petersburg, thanks to what looked like a new ownership group from Florida. But Peter Magowan, CEO of supermarket chain Safeway, came in with a higher bid and kept the team in San Francisco. Not only that, Magowan hired good baseball people—GM Brian Sabean, managers Dusty Baker and Felipe Alou—and let them do their thing: They created a winning franchise. Magowan also built the first privately financed baseball park since 1962, the beautiful Pac Bell (now SBC Park), which raised annual revenues by about $100 million. And one of his first moves was to spend big bucks on free agent Barry Bonds, shortly after buying the ballclub. In short, Magowan, a hands-on managing partner, didn't just save baseball in San Francisco—he brought it to a level of greatness it hadn't seen before.

■ Ewing Kauffman (Royals)

Kauffman, who made his fortune in the pharmaceuticals business, owned the expansion Royals from 1969 until his death in 1993. By 1976, he had built a great new stadium and an extraordinarily popular (and winning) team. Kauffman didn't know about "small market"—he knew Kansas City was his town, and spent, big time, to ensure a winning franchise. Kauffman wasn't just a winner— "Mr. K" was a beloved civic treasure, a man who gave millions and millions to charity and lost millions and millions on the Royals, because he cared more about people than about money.

Kareem and his preceptor
"I always coached the unspectacular *in basketball,*" says John Wooden.

people are beginning to suggest that the negative effects of our highlight culture go way beyond sports. "Some say that showing all those dunks and jams on *SportsCenter* has changed the way that basketball is played," says James Steyer, a professor of constitutional law at Stanford and CEO of Common Sense Media. "But what's more important, I think, is the effect it has on kids. Kids use what they see on TV as a metaphor for interpreting the world around them. And when they see this focus on individual play, they come to think that's how they'll get ahead in life." Andy Hill, former president of CBS Productions (and an end-of-the-bench player for Wooden at UCLA), goes further still. "I'm not saying you need to turn ESPN into *Touched by an Angel,*" says Hill, who developed that show along with *Walker, Texas Ranger; Caroline in the City* and many others. "I love *SportsCenter,* and I watch it all the time. But you need to keep in mind the influence and power you have over the hopes and expectations of young people. We are becoming a culture of 'I'—everything is I, I, I, except when it's me, me, me. Now, I'm not suggesting that ESPN alone is responsible for this; but I do think ESPN's highlights are right at the top of the problem list."

Whew. Not everyone at ESPN agrees with that; but almost everyone *does* seem aware of the problem and agrees with Levy that "we do have to accept some of the responsibility." From time to time, Patrick has declared a "No Dunk Night" on *SportsCenter* to emphasize other aspects of the sport. And the network does produce some highlights that not only demonstrate the importance of teamwork, but glorify it. Such highlights can be tough to pull off, though, and often need a tremendous amount of enthusiasm from a narrator, not only to explain precisely what's going on, but to color in the drama. Stuart Scott's narration of what he called a "sweet little back-door play" by Memphis against Louisville—a play that would certainly have been overlooked by a network with no appreciation of the team game—is a fine example of what's required.

The highlight begins with an isolation on Alex Sanders, who's cut off by a solid back-screen that starts the Memphis offense. Scott points out how all the Memphis players move without the ball, setting up Marcus Moody for the score. But what makes the highlight delicious—that is, what makes it good TV, as well as good hoops—is less the play itself than Scott's enjoyment of it. "Moody makes it through the back door, into the backyard," he hoots. And as the ball goes down, Scott goes over the top to make his point: "Everybody shares!

Horn on the horn *Highlight-driven egomania reached an NFL low in 2003 when Joe Horn pretended to place a phone call after catching a touchdown pass. Some criticized Horn, pointing out that he must have known this display would cost his team 15 yards, but didn't care. Others disagreed, arguing that Horn evidently didn't understand the word "team" at all.*

Somebody's playin' some Funkadelic on the 8-track. Everybody's sippin' Kool-Aid, a little sugar at the bottom! It's cool."

It is worth noting that while not everyone appreciates the shtick that ESPN's anchors ladle out, sometimes it serves a definite purpose . . . and this is clearly one of those times. Let's face it: Teamwork may taste like sugar at the bottom, but it doesn't always look as good as it tastes.

Many at ESPN hasten to point out that if basketball highlights have a tendency to aggrandize selfish play, other sports are less likely affected. No matter how desperately a third baseman may want to see himself on *SportsCenter*, there's not much he can do to cut his teammates out of a double play. And yet, baseball analyst Harold Reynolds, for one, sees room for improvement in other sports as well.

"I grew up with the Baseball Bunch," he says, fondly remembering the little lessons in fundamentals that used to appear on *This Week in Baseball*. "If you're a kid watching TV today, you don't get that kind of teaching anywhere. We certainly don't do it in our highlights. I wish we did." And one more thing: celebrations. "There's a difference between a natural expression of joy, which is fine," says Reynolds, "and calling attention to yourself, which is not."

Such celebrations are taking a toll on NFL play. Indeed, on a single weekend in 2003, three different players sabatoged their sport by indulging in childish, self-aggrandizing antics. Patriots cornerback Tyrone Poole intercepted a Jacksonville pass and then, thinking he had clear sailing to the end zone, slowed down and waved the ball over his head like a kid with a new toy. He didn't see Jaguars tailback LaBrandon Toefield closing in on him. Not only did Poole fail to score, Toefield nearly stripped the ball. Meanwhile, Falcons running back T.J. Duckett was in Indianapolis, celebrating a touchdown with a merry dance—though his team still trailed the Colts by no less than 25 points. ESPN's Sean Salisbury wondered if this sort of "never-mind-the-score-look-how-great-I-am" attitude might explain the Falcons' worst-in the-league record. But the capper came in New Orleans, where Saints receiver Joe Horn paid homage to his magnificent self by pretending to place a call on his cell phone after a TD. Sure, it cost his team 15 yards. But Horn was too selfish to care.

"We shouldn't even *show* stuff like that," fumes Reynolds. "Why encourage it? I mean, we don't show streakers."

But maybe that's because Horn hasn't tried streaking yet. ∎

"Every night I tell myself, 'I'm going to dream about my girl, I'm going to dream about my girl.' But it's always ham hocks."
—Cowboys 320-pound offensive lineman Nate Newton

CHAPTER 7

Piling On and Rubbing It In

THERE IS, OF COURSE, ANOTHER WAY IN WHICH HIGHLIGHTS can hurt: when they deride the athletes pictured in them. Perhaps this seems obvious; and yet, there is something about sports that can make ordinary, decent people go completely off their nuts, and forget that a human heart beats beneath every jersey. This is not to suggest that athletes should be immune from criticism, only that such criticism should be thoughtful, compassionate and just.

In his eight years as a running back with the Steelers and Bears, Merril Hoge never made anyone forget Franco Harris or Walter Payton. But he was a famously balls-out player whose battering-ram style left him with as many concussions as yards gained. To this day, nothing seems to gall him more than the hustle-challenged prima donnas who occasionally crop up in professional sports. Such players are almost always endowed with remarkable talent. After all, how else would they ever get away with their dogging? To a player like Hoge, who wrung every last droplet of football productivity from his far more limited gifts, such waste is just sinful. That is why Hoge, now cohost of *NFL Matchup*, was destined to lock horns with Vikings receiver Randy Moss in September 2000.

Moss had caught just 12 passes in his first three games of that season, and Hoge was curious about what might be holding him back. He studied every play Moss had run in the

Mismeasure of a man *Replays of Bill Buckner's 1986 World Series boot were so relentless, the play unjustly overshadows his career to this day.*

"We can't win at home. We can't win on the road . . . As general manager, I just can't figure out where else to play."

—Pat Williams, Orlando Magic general manager, after his team got off to a 7-27 start in 1992

Lighting his fire After ESPN analyst Merril Hoge showed negative highlights of Randy Moss's listless play, the Vikings receiver delivered a breakout performance.

previous week and was flabbergasted by what he found. "Thirty-four legitimate plays where Moss either stood there, walked or jogged," said Hoge. "Even once or twice is too much." So Hoge went on *NFL Matchup* and uncorked a hellaciously negative highlight. There was Moss, down after down, loping around the field with all the enthusiasm of a teenager doing his Sunday chores. Hoge said it didn't matter how talented Moss was; as long as he played like that, there were at least 20 NFL receivers who were more valuable to their teams.

Now, surely, Dr. Phil would have urged Hoge to deliver his constructive criticisms to Moss in a more nurturing manner. On the other hand, Bill Parcells might have found Hoge's tone far too pantywaist. But regardless of how he said it, Hoge's negative highlight was unassailable on moral grounds. The same certainly cannot be said about all negative highlights. Simple decency ought to tell us that it is almost always wrong

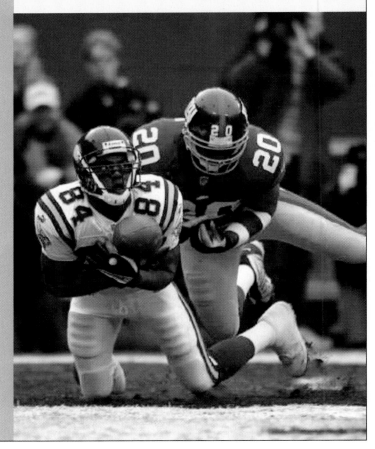

to criticize a player who tries to do his best, but fails. (Life, after all, is a game in which we struggle to survive, but ultimately fail; there's no shame in it.) Equally execrable are those highlights that heap derision on a player who makes a thoroughly human mental error in a pressure-filled situation. But on this occasion, Hoge did none of that: He simply held up a mirror to a player who seemed to have made a deliberate decision to disrespect his coaches, his teammates and, worst of all, his sport.

Moss, apparently, had a different opinion about this and he made that opinion clear to his teammates. Offensive tackle Todd Steussie replied by getting in Moss's face and, in the words of another teammate, giving him a lotta "stuff." Veteran receiver Cris Carter confessed that he, too, "challenged" Moss, as he put it, to "play a complete game . . . to run . . . to put pressure on them." Moss responded by catching seven passes for 168 yards and three touchdowns—and, better yet, throwing an ungodly open-field block to spring Robert Smith for a 65-yard touchdown run.

Afterwards, Moss was understandably reluctant to admit that Hoge's negative highlight had anything to do with his breakout performance. "I don't want to tell you it was a big motivation," he told reporters, "but at the same time, *it was the first time I've ever heard somebody criticize me*." And that's why the negative highlight is sometimes both necessary and, ultimately, positive: Some people have ears, but neither do they hear. You have to show 'em. "I do believe I saw Randy Moss play every play," Hoge chuckled afterwards. "And when he plays like that, nobody can touch him."

How would you like a job," the late Hall of Fame goalie Jacques Plante once asked, "where, every time you make a mistake, someone turns a light on and 18,000 people boo?"

It's a good question, except that it doesn't go nearly far enough. Try this: How would you like a job where, after 18,000 people have booed their guts out at you, your mistake is then replayed on television before millions more—not once, but over and over again—as witty television personalities make wisecracks about what a dunderhead you are, about what you *should* have done, about how there *must* be someone out there who could do your job better than you're doing it?

You would not like it. Nor do professional athletes, for

> **"There's only about 5,000 of them, how can you miss? You can hear somebody all the way up in the upper deck. It's sad."**
>
> —Barry Bonds, responding to a question about whether he heard Pirates fans booing when he returned to Pittsburgh as a Giant

■ Over the past 25 years, we've been blessed with enough great sports books to fill . . . well, a book bag. None of us have read them all (although we'd love to have the time), but all of the contributors to this list have their own (strong) opinions. So we came up with a master list consisting of dozens and dozens of sports books, focusing on those that are good reads (thereby arbitrarily eliminating some great reference books that have come out lately). And then we put them to a vote of ESPN literary aficionados. It's pure (happy) happenstance that seven different sports are represented.

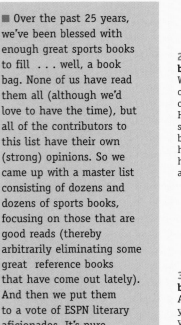

1. Friday Night Lights: A Town, a Team, and a Dream by H. G. Bissinger (1990)
The town is Odessa, a boom-and-bust oil town in western Texas. The team is the Permian High School Panthers, the winningest team in state history. The dream? Living life, between September and December, with the whole town focused on teenagers who may (but probably won't) go on to further greatness. Bissinger's classic details some of the uglier aspects of American sports in the modern age.

2. Seabiscuit by Laura Hillenbrand (2001)
Who would've believed that the story of a 1930s racehorse would have captivated millions and become a Hollywood blockbuster? Huge sales and show business glitz don't make this book great, though—the magic is in how Hillenbrand brings an obscure horse, and lots of forgotten history, alive again.

3. King of the World by David Remnick (1998)
As Remnick follows the progress of a young Cassius Clay, from brash young Olympic champ to a world heavyweight champ who insisted on being called by his new Muslim name, he also explains the making of a cultural icon. The general career arc of Ali is well known, but how the man created of himself a true original is a mysterious process, probably even to Ali himself. Remnick, in this brilliantly written short biography, makes sense of it all, never forgetting that while Ali helped shape American culture, it also shaped Ali.

4. Moneyball by Michael Lewis (2003)
A you-are-there, behind-the-scenes account of how A's GM Billy Beane is revolutionizing baseball with a little bit of money, a lot of sabermetric stats and gobs of smart. A compelling read that blends baseball and business in a more interesting fashion than most thought possible.

5. Into Thin Air by John Krakauer (1997)
A controversial account of the disastrous 1996 Everest climbing season, written by an experienced mountaineer who summited as a storm that killed five climbers raged beneath him. Krakauer wrote his first account for *Outside* magazine, then quickly expanded it into a book. But he wasn't just padding. For one thing, he closely examined his own role in the catastrophe—and found his own actions wanting. Then he talked to many others, and painted a complex picture of heroism and cowardice, good and bad decisions and an overcrowded mountain, all of which played a part in the disaster.

6. A Season on the Brink by John Feinstein (1989)
According to Amazon.com, it's the best-selling sports book of all time. But that's not what makes it great. It's the definitive look inside the world Bob Knight created, because of the incredible access Knight gave Feinstein during the 1985-86 season. Feinstein saw it all, captured it all, then somehow made sense of one of the most brilliant and baffling coaches of this era.

7. The Bill James Historical Baseball Abstract (1985) / The New Bill James Historical Baseball Abstract (2001)
James is a thinker and historian who writes with clarity, simplicity and wit, proving that baseball stats can be a

lively starting point for baseball reading—and conversation. His "Decade in a Box" lists are witty and provocative, and his player rankings—by position, the top 100 of all time—will surprise. The "New" version, published in 2001, contains huge amounts of new material.

8. Joe DiMaggio: The Hero's Life by Richard Ben Cramer (2000)

The man and the myth, warts included. Cramer's biography reflects a great respect for DiMaggio's abilities on the field, but calls into question just about everything else in his life—his rocky beginnings with the Yankees, his thirst for money, his failed marriages. It's all there, including a panicked Joe D. running into his house during the 1989 San Francisco earthquake to rescue garbage bags full of cash.

9. When Pride Still Mattered by David Maraniss (2000)

Forget about hero worship here—Maraniss goes way beyond hagiography to explore all the nuances of the complex man who was Lombardi. The chapters covering his Packer years are fascinating, especially the relationships he created with players like Paul Hornung. And the examination of Lombardi's off-field life—his often-difficult marriage, his friendships and rivalries, and his religion—is definitive.

10. The Breaks of the Game by David Halberstam (1981)

Halberstam chronicles a season with the 1979-80 Trail Blazers, and somehow covers it all—the players, the front office, the media, the money, race and politics. Halberstam's book provided a great landscape portrait of a particular game/business and place at a time when the sports world was undergoing all kinds of radical changes.

11. Game Time: A Baseball Companion by Roger Angell (2003)

Angell is, simply, the best pure writer on baseball. His *New Yorker* articles lead readers, carefully and compellingly, into new ways of thinking about the game and the people who inhabit it. Just about any collection of Angell's *New Yorker* pieces will do, but this, the most recent, covers the most fun things to read about—the swing of Ted Williams, the pitching form of Tom Seaver, Barry Bonds at Pac Bell, and even a scout scouring rural Kentucky.

12. Fever Pitch by Nick Hornby (1994)

Hornby, an incredibly successful fiction writer (*About a Boy*, *High Fidelity*), became an Arsenal fanatic in 1968, when his father first took him to a game as a way for the two to "bond." What happened next his father didn't exactly expect—Arsenal football took over the 11-year-old boy's life. And it has con-

sumed him for at least the next 24 years (when the book ends).

13. The Curious Case of Sidd Finch by George Plimpton (1987)

You'll know from the start of this book that Sidd Finch is a fictional character, but plenty of *Sports Illustrated* readers who first heard of the hurler in April (as in "fools") 1985 didn't. The hilarious tale of a Buddhist monk turned fireballer, with a deadly accurate 168 mph fastball. Will he be the Mets' next franchise pitcher?

14. Dollar Sign on the Muscle by Kevin Kerrane (1984)

Kerrane's book sheds light on a well-known but little-explored part of baseball—the semisystematic discovery of talent, and the men who make a living scouring the country for "the next (insert name here)."

15. Nine Innings by Daniel Okrent (1984)

On June 10, 1982, the Brewers and Orioles played a single game that would have been quickly forgotten were it not for Okrent's play-by-play analysis. It's not just pitch, hit, field (although the detail makes the book unique)—Okrent digresses wonderfully, writing about signals, pitching mechanics, the history of the slider, and the dollars behind it all.

Somebody else's troubles Highlights of Jacque Vaughn's shooting slump were hilarious— until you realized that Vaughn might have feelings.

whom the Negative Highlight is an occupational hazard. Sports journalists, and fans, often find comfort in the presumption that jocks are 10 feet tall and bulletproof, that they barely hear the boos and the jibes flung at them—a presumption often bolstered by athletes themselves, most of whom are too macho to let their "weaknesses" show. Say something hurtful about 'em and they might get *angry* and crack your head open. But *wounded? Distraught? Depressed?* No way.

"Bullshit," says ESPN football analyst Sean Salisbury, a former NFL quarterback who has heard the I'm-too-tough-to-let-it-bother-me speech from athletes more often than he can count. "Athletes are the most sensitive people on earth. They hear every 'boo'. I know I did." With this in mind, consider the following NBA highlight from a *SportsCenter* of recent mint.

"It hasn't been a great start of the season for Jacque Vaughn," begins the voiceover. "He's had a little trouble shooting so far." Poor Vaughn is shown taking jumper after jumper, aiming each one with intense concentration, like a small boy trying to write the letter "S" for the first time. Shots fall short, sail wide and clank off the rim. As it turns out, Vaughn is an incredible 0-for-22 from the field coming into the game. Now a shot chart appears on screen, heartlessly showing every spot from which Vaughn has missed. Cut to tonight's game: "That's Jacque Vaughn," says the voiceover, as the guard moves energetically on offense, looking for a pass. "Wide open—probably for a reason—begging for the ball." Vaughn stands just beyond the arc, waving his arms wildly above his head, the way your little brother used to do when your mom made you promise to let him play with you and your friends at the park. Vaughn's teammates appear to be doing exactly what you did: pretending not to see him. "Jacque Vaughn had no shots in the first quarter," says the voiceover. "Second quarter, Jacque Vaughn in the lane"—he's got a clear path to the basket; he goes up for the lay-in; the voiceover trembles with mock emotion and then shouts: "*IT GOES!!!!*" Suddenly, the game disappears, and fireworks explode across the screen, Beethoven's Ninth Symphony swells triumphantly and crowds of people celebrate; bulls run through the streets of Pamplona. Jacque Vaughn has scored at last! Basketball returns to the screen. "Later in the second," says the voiceover, Vaughn gets free for a short easy jumper—but it clanks away miserably. "We're back to old times," sighs the voice. "Darn. I wanted to see the running of the bulls again."

Now, it's awfully hard to watch this highlight without at least grinning, even if you happen to be related to Vaughn. Part of what makes it funny is that, metaphorically speaking, we've all been exactly where Jacque Vaughn found himself, trying and trying, and failing and failing, and trying again. We're laughing at him, yes, but unless we have very little self-awareness, we ought to be laughing at ourselves, too.

At the same time, there's no denying the whole thing was "a little mean-spirited," as Vaughn's teammate Emanual Davis put it. Vaughn's response could not have left anyone at ESPN feeling terribly proud. "I didn't really know how to react," he told a reporter after seeing the tape. "I've always been good to those guys. So I guess I'm surprised." This was not some egomaniac who had never heard anyone criticize him before, just an ordinary guy who had been playing his heart out every night and coming up short—and whose feelings were hurt because people he'd never wronged were making fun of him. Granted, as media crimes go, this one was awfully small. Bruised feelings and public humiliation are the price of playing on any big stage. But "when boys throw stones at frogs for fun," the ancient proverb goes, "the frogs die in earnest." If you're in the highlight business, that's worth remembering.

In this regard, sports reporters can be remarkably insensitive. When John Kasay muffed a kickoff in the waning moments of Super Bowl XXXVIII, his gaffe was jeered mercilessly. "Not every kicker can pick the worst time of his career to kick the ball out of bounds," spat a commentator on ESPN.com. Of course, Kasay had not "chosen" the moment at random; he'd made the error in one of the most high-pressure situations of his life. Moreover, the repeated replays of his error helped fans forget that Kasay had also nailed a 50-yarder as time expired at halftime, while Patriots kicker Adam Vinatieri had missed two far easier kicks. In other words, Carolina was only in a position to win it at the end *because of*

Most Lopsided Trades

■ Since the advent of free agency and salary caps, trades have become much more complicated. We chose the most lopsided by looking, in retrospect, at exchanges in which one team clearly—often overwhelmingly—got an extraordinary deal. The circumstances of the trades vary tremendously, but in general, two types of trades were omitted: those that were forced by the players (like when Kobe Bryant, drafted by the Hornets, refused to play for Charlotte) or "salary dumps" (when teams knowingly took lesser players in order to reduce payroll).

1. Cowboys send Herschel Walker to Vikings for five players, a 1992 draft pick and six conditional draft choices (1989)
Walker played two-plus years for the Vikings, averaging about four yards per carry—decent, but not great. His best season for the Vikes came in 1991, when he rushed for 825 yards. Minnesota then said goodbye rather than pay Walker $1.7 million the following year. In the meantime, the Boys used two of their newly acquired draft picks on Emmitt Smith and Darren Woodson, offensive and defensive cornerstones of Cowboys teams that won three Super Bowls in four seasons.

2. Falcons send Brett Favre to Packers for No. 1 draft pick (1992)
The Falcons thought Favre was too undisciplined, too much of a party guy, and also thought they were set at QB with Chris Miller, a 26-year-old who'd been a Pro Bowler in 1991 and also led the Falcons to the playoffs. Favre turned into a three-time MVP, perhaps the greatest

continued on page 122

continued from page 121

QB ever. Miller injured his knee and wouldn't play for Atlanta after 1993. The No. 1 draft pick? Tony Smith, a running back who played 33 games in three seasons.

3. Colts send John Elway to Broncos for Mark Herrmann, Chris Hinton and a 1984 first-round draft pick (1983)

The Colts took the Stanford QB as the first overall pick in 1983, but he refused to sign with Baltimore. So the Colts traded him to the Broncos, where he went on to play for 16 years, throwing for 51,475 yards (second most in NFL history), tossing 300 TD passes (third in NFL history), appearing in five Super Bowls and winning two. Hinton, a five-time All-Pro tackle, played seven years with the Colts. Herrmann, a QB, played only five games with the Colts. The first-round draft pick in 1984 turned out to be guard Ron Solt, who played five seasons with the Colts.

4. Celtics send No. 1 and No. 13 1980 draft picks to Warriors for Robert Parish and No. 3 1980 draft pick.

The Celts' No. 3 pick turned out to be Kevin McHale, one of the top 50 players in NBA history. Between them Parish and McHale won three titles and reached the NBA finals five times with Boston. Golden State selected Joe Barry Carroll as the No. 1 pick, who played well during six seasons with Golden State, averaging 24.1 ppg in 1982–83. The No. 13 pick was guard Rickey Brown, a reserve who played five NBA seasons. While Parish and McHale teamed up with Larry Bird to make history, the Warriors only made the playoffs once during Carroll's tenure.

5. Bulls send Olden Polynice and a second-round pick to the SuperSonics for Scottie Pippen (1987)

A draft-night deal that cemented the Bulls championship run, as Pippen, one of the top 50 players in NBA history, and MJ meshed in Chicago. In 15 seasons,

Kasay's superior kicking. But you never would have known it from watching ESPN's highlights.

The best way to understand how hurtful a negative highlight can be is to talk to *retired* athletes, as they are more likely to have set aside the mask of invulnerability that most jocks feel their jobs require. Wally Henry, a former Pro Bowl kick return specialist, is best remembered for fumbling two kicks in a 1981 playoff game against the Giants. Why? Highlights.

"Normally, when you have a big boo-boo, you go out to the parking lot and you get some suds and hope it will blow over," he says, without bitterness or regret. "Then you can come back and make a big play and everyone will love you again. But it never did blow over, not that time. When the media decides to sell a story, to dramatize it on tape, well, you have no chance. It's always gonna be in the VCR, and that's how people will remember it. And that's how they'll remember you."

Or to put it another way, that's how they'll *misremember* you. The late Stephen Jay Gould, paleontologist, baseball fan and scholar of what he liked to call the "mismeasure of man," often used sports to illustrate a common flaw in human cognition. Who doesn't remember Bill Buckner's error in the 1986 World Series, when a routine grounder off Mookie Wilson's bat rolled through his legs? But Gould noted a widely held belief—among *journalists*, as well as fans—that this error occurred when the Red Sox were "one out away from winning the championship." Actually, the score was tied and the game was an out away from extra innings. Beyond that, the constant repetition of this highlight has overwhelmed Buckner's brilliant 22-year career, his 2,715 hits and, for the most part, superb defense. One negative highlight can rob a player of his hard-earned identity. That, too, is worth remembering.

Mike McQuade always tries to remember these things, but in the end, he says, "I don't think we have any idea how athletes are affected by highlights—how they *feel*. Most of the time, we're completely glowing, just savoring what they do. But there are times when we pile on, too, and we can be cruel. We talk about it; but maybe not as much as we should."

How *do* they feel? How did it feel, for instance, to be Trey Junkin, who was, without question, one of the best long-snappers in football for some 9 years. In that time, Junkin muffed just half a dozen snaps, and it was precisely because of his long record of excellence that the New York Giants signed him up late in the 2002 season. Alas, his seventh muff came with time running out in a playoff game against the 49ers. There is no point in repeating what was said as the highlights rolled, over and over and over again. Just about everyone was cruel, but the New York media, famous for giving no quarter, lived up to its reputation in spades. Now, to return to our question: How does it feel?

"I doubt I've actually seen the entire play on TV more than twice," says Junkin today, from his quiet home in Louisiana. "There is an 'off' button on the TV and I've used it many times. But I don't need a TV to see that highlight; all I have to do is close my eyes." And when he does, he is flooded with nausea, dizziness and "that sick feeling where your chest gets tight and you can't breathe. It's the same feeling I had while the play was going on. I still wake up at night to it. I can still get wrapped up in it just driving down the road."

That is how it feels; and that, too, is worth remembering. Junkin, a man blessed with a fine sense of perspective, and of humor, craves no sympathy. "I made a mistake. I made a bad snap and I accept full responsibility. But does that snap define me as a man? No. What defines me is the way I approached the game, with hard work and attention to detail.

Polynice, an NBA journeyman, averaged 7.8 points and 6.7 rebounds per game.

6. A's send Mark McGwire to Cardinals for pitchers T. J. Mathews, Eric Ludwick and Blake Stein (1997)

A deadline trade—McGwire's contract was about to expire, and the A's didn't even want to hear what the "hometown price" would be. But it was still a bad move. McGwire hit 24 dingers for the Cards in 1997, and 196 more thereafter, electrifying fans in 1998 when he broke Maris's record. The Cards: 220 homers and a likeable superstar. The A's? Ludwick went from bad (1-4, 8.25 ERA in August and September 1997) to worse. Stein and Mathews were gone from the A's long before McGwire hung it up.

continued on page 124

Electric chair or firing squad? With a Giants' season in the balance against the 49ers, center Trey Junkin muffed the snap on Matt Bryant's field goal attempt. The highlight-driven roasting that followed was so frenzied, some might have wondered why Junkin hadn't been arrested.

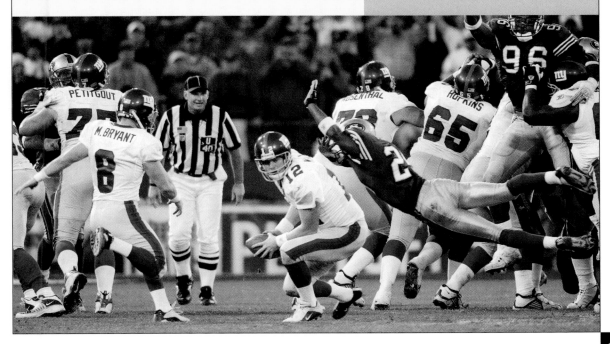

continued from page 123

7. Bucs send Steve Young to 49ers for second and fourth-round picks (1987)
Tampa Bay gets a couple of draft choices. The Niners get a great backup for Joe Montana, a great student, and, eventually, one of the greatest QBs of all time.

8. White Sox send Sammy Sosa and Ken Patterson to Cubs for George Bell (1992)
Bell played well for the White Sox in 1992 (25 HR, 112 RBI), but was out of baseball after the Chisox released him following the 1993 season (knee surgery/bad attitude). Patterson, a reliever, had an undistinguished season with the Cubs before heading to the Angels. Sammy's headed to the HOF.

9. Blackhawks send Dominik Hasek to the Sabres for backup goalie Stéphane Beauregard and a fourth-round draft pick (1992)
Hasek: NHL MVP, 1997 and 1998; six-time Vezina Trophy winner. Beauregard: Spent most of his time with teams like the Moncton Hawks, Springfield Falcons, San Francisco Spiders, Quebec Rafales, Chicago Wolves and Schwenningen Wild Wings.

10. Phillies send Ryne Sandberg and Larry Bowa to Cubs for Ivan DeJesus (1982)
Sandberg had played only 13 games for the Phillies in 1981, his first call-up to the bigs, before being dealt. Three years later, he was NL MVP. A perennial All-Star and Gold Glover, he is on his way to the Hall of Fame. The aging Bowa played 3 $\frac{1}{2}$ so-so seasons for the Cubs. DeJesus, a 29-year-old shortstop, played only marginally better in his three seasons with the Phillies. So, Bowa and DeJesus canceled each other out. And the Cubbies got a great player for free.

That's who I am, and there's a whole lot more to me than football." He also understands why his blunder produced such a highlight frenzy. "It sells. I mean, how many times can they show John Elway throwing touchdowns? Everybody loves to see people falling on their asses." But it still hurts, and it probably always will. "A really good friend who's a behavioral psychologist told me, 'It will fade in time.' Well, I'm waiting for it to fade. And it's not fading."

No name troubles the conscience of sports media more than Donnie Moore. Moore, of course, was an All-Star reliever for the California Angels who pitched manfully, but ineffectively, in one of the greatest games ever played. His failure was replayed relentlessly on television, as such failures are, and the fans never forgave Moore for being human. They jeered him every time he stuck his nose out of the bullpen. And then, in 1989, Moore snapped, fired a gun at his wife, wounding her, and then committed suicide.

Let us be clear: Moore's suicide was caused neither by the media, nor the fans. He was tormented by demons without number—money problems, family issues and relentless depression. It was his demons that killed him. But to face such anguish every day, knowing the whole world looks at you and sees failure—that is not a fate to wish on anyone. Certainly, Donnie Moore did not deserve it. He ought to have been remembered as an actor in a classic sports drama.

The Big A was packed and seething on October 12, 1986, and Red Sox DH Don Baylor was standing on first base. Angels infielder Bobby Grich was holding him on. The two warriors had come up together in the Orioles organization some 20 years before and were nearing the end of their careers. Between them, they'd played in more than 4,000 major league games, so it really meant something when Baylor turned to Grich and said: "This is the greatest game I've ever played in."

"Same for me, buddy," Grich agreed.

The Red Sox had started the day down three games to one in the American League Championship Series and the Curse of the Bambino looked to be in full flower. In the fifth inning, with the Sox up 2-1, Boston center fielder Tony Armas twisted his ankle and was replaced by Dave Henderson. In the sixth, Grich hit a deep fly ball to left center. Henderson chased it to the warning track and reached up. "I thought I had it all the way," he later said, "but my wrist hit the top of the wall and knocked

Bad day at the office *Angels coach Marcel Lachemann tried to console closer Donnie Moore after a playoff gopher ball in 1986. But unforgiving highlights kept the memory fresh, and California fans never forgave him. Three years later, troubled by family and financial woes, Moore committed suicide.*

the ball out of the park . . . I should have caught it." Sox pitcher Bruce Hurst was so horrified that he literally fell down.

And that's the most remarkable, long-forgotten fact about that historic, tragic contest: Henderson could easily have been the goat. Had the dice tumbled differently, Henderson might have spent the rest of his life watching that highlight in agony. It could have been one of the worst days of his life—instead of one of the best. In sports, and especially in baseball, glory and humiliation are two opposite ends of one great hermaphroditic beast, and you never know which end is going to bite you.

The Sox were down 5-2 in the top of the ninth and Angels starter Mike Witt was cruising. But Baylor came to the plate with one out and a runner on and crushed a two-run homer. Suddenly, the game was within reach, for the next batter was the great Jim Rice. But Rice popped out weakly. Smelling triumph, Angels manager Gene Mauch sent pitching coach Marcel Lachemann out to get Witt, because the next batter, Boston catcher Rich Gedman, had been hitting him hard all afternoon. In came lefty Gary Lucas, known for his pin-point control. In more than 400 innings, he had never beaned a

Best Promotions

■ Gimmicks and giveaways designed to lure fans into parks and arenas have long been a staple of sports. Ladies Days and memorabilia handouts always drew big crowds. But over the past quarter century, owners have had to work even harder to gain fans' attention. Discounted seats, fireworks, bobblehead dolls and postgame concerts are cool. But some teams have raised clever promotions to an art form, garnering extra publicity (highlight-reel kudos) by coming up with innovative ways to involve fans. Or, in Mike Veeck's case—for one night, at least—keep fans away.

1. Seat Cushion Night (St. Paul Saints)

On June 7, 2002, with talk of a baseball strike going strong, the St. Paul Saints gave away seat cushions with Bud Selig on one side and MLBPA chief Don Fehr on the other. As fans relaxed in soft comfort, they also cast a vote for the man they liked least—and as it turned out, 90 percent were sitting on Selig's face.

2. Ted Williams Popsicle Night
(Bisbee-Douglas Copper Kings)

With the dead baseball great frozen in nearby Scottsdale, John Guy, part owner and GM of the Copper Kings, decided to honor Williams's memory by celebrating his cryogenic state. Hence, the first 500 fans to enter the home ballpark of the Arizona-Mexico League for the June 2, 2003, game got a treat—a popsicle. It was that simple... and that clever.

3. Arthur Andersen Night
(Portland Beavers)

In 2002, the Triple-A Portland Beavers had "Arthur Andersen Night" in appreciation of the scandal-mired accounting firm that helped bring down the owner of their stadium's sponsor, PGE. Everyone named

hitter. But damned if Lucas's first-pitch fastball didn't plunk Gedman on the ear. Henderson was waiting on deck. "Gedman was laying down on the plate and normally you would see if the guy was okay," he remembers. "But I stepped right over him and tried to get into the batter's box." Mauch quickly retrieved the shaken Lucas and called for his door slammer, Donnie Moore.

Moore never revealed what he was thinking as he made his way to the mound. He was a 31-year-old right-hander coming off an All-Star season in 1985 when he'd notched 31 saves and a 1.92 ERA. That performance had earned him a multimillion-dollar contract, top price in those days. But the '86 season had been an excruciating struggle: His shoulder, his rib cage and his back were shot to hell with injuries. He needed rest.

"I went, 'Oh, no!'" remembers Angels third baseman Doug DeCinces as Moore marched to the mound. "And I think everybody on our team went, 'Oh no!'" Moore had received a cortisone shot after the Angels' victory the previous night. "And anybody who's had a cortisone shot knows there's no physical way you can perform, especially in less than 24 hours," says DeCinces. "Donnie Moore was a tough cookie, but nobody is that tough. He always just took the ball no matter what, which is a credit to him but . . . he had absolutely nothing."

By this time, Witt was in the locker room, "juicing my arm, getting ready for, I don't know, the World Series." There was champagne waiting in a cooler and the lockers were covered with tarps to protect them from the spray. Don Drysdale was waiting to do the triumphal postgame interviews.

Moore's pitching style was no mystery. "The pitch that made him was a forkball," remembers his catcher, Bob Boone. "But when he had the back problem . . . he didn't always throw it with the same arm action. He would push some. And even if it was in a real good spot, as a hitter, you could see it."

Witt remembers the rhythm of Henderson's at-bat perfectly: "Fastball, forkball, fastball, forkball." The count went to two-and-two. The Angels were a strike away from the pennant. And Henderson stepped out of the box, to prepare himself for the moment that would ineffably shape the lives of two men, himself and Donnie Moore.

"We're ballplayers, so we fail most of the time," Henderson would say in the clubhouse when it was all over. "You have to learn to cope with it. . . . I had to step out of the box and gather myself." So before stepping in to face Moore, he did something that amazed everyone: He yawned. More than a decade later, he was still chuckling about it. "When you get adrenalated and really excited, everybody says: Take deep breaths. That doesn't work. I took a big yawn. A yawn is the closest thing to going to sleep, to settle you down. I yawned and looked at the fans. They were in their starter's box, ready to run out onto the field when I struck out."

Of course, he did not strike out. He took Moore's next pitch, a forkball, and smoked it out of the Big A for a 6-5 lead. He rounded the bases thinking of when he was a kid in his backyard fantasizing about hitting a home run, just like this one. "And I actually hit the home run in front of 60 million people watching. . . I actually did it on TV!"

Of course, Moore had done something on TV, too: He had failed. No one fantasizes about that. In the locker room, Witt sat stunned: "The camera left, the champagne left."

A sad time for the losers, certainly. But there was no reason for anyone connected with that game to feel shame. And yet, derision was hurled at Moore as rice is hurled at newlyweds. He never did recover from his injuries, or from the storms of abuse that seemed to reignite every time the replay rolled. "Highlights, the media—you can't blame them for his death," says Brian Downing, one of his closest friends. "Ninety percent of what troubled him had nothing to do with baseball." But if you take someone who's emotionally fragile, if you goad him and harass him, and replay his failures on television over and over again—well, don't you run the risk of pushing him over the edge?

"That pretty much encapsulates the whole thing," says Downing. "We always used to stretch down the left field line, and he'd talk about it all the time. It bothered him. Bothered him so much. He'd tell me: 'Someday, I'm going to climb up that foul pole and jump off.'"

Nobody wanted Moore to do that. And Moore's father, Conaway, is adamant that the reasons for his son's death were manifold and complex. "Did baseball kill my son?" he recently told the *Denver Post*. "No, sir."

But Americans have come to love highlights because highlights are powerful, because they stir both our insatiable appetite for entertainment and certain heroic mythologies that are part of our ancient heritage. Like fire or muscle, or anything powerful, a highlight can produce awe and wonder—or, it can burn and wound. ∎

Arthur or Andersen got in free, and shredding stations were spread throughout the stadium. Naturally, the "accounting" of the night's attendance was inflated, reflecting Andersen's problems with basic accounting. Attendance was announced as 58,667—about three times capacity. And, surprisingly enough, home runs went a lot farther than usual—it was 1,317 feet down the left field line, 1,405 to center, and 1,320 to right. And everyone was a winner, tax deduction wise. Fans who bought $5 tickets got receipts for $10.

4. Nobody Night (Charleston RiverDogs)
One of innovative owner Mike Veeck's more imaginative schemes. On July 8,

2002, the gates in Charleston were padlocked as the RiverDogs took on the Columbus Redstixx. A huge party was held outside the ballpark as the RiverDogs attempted to break the record for lowest attendance at a game, said to be the 12 who saw Chicago defeat Troy on September 17, 1881. The gates held tight until after the fifth inning, when the new record—zero—became official.

5. Flash-Card Football (Portland State)
In the first game of the Portland State Vikings' 1989 season, 1,500 fans with flash cards voted on whether the Vikings, playing against Cameron University (Lawton, Oklahoma), should run or pass during a series of downs in the third quarter. Most fans voted for a pass, and it was complete. Then the fans voted for a run, on which the Vikings scored a TD. "If they can do that every time, they can keep calling them," said offensive coordinator Al Borges. Portland State won, 35-21.

Next...

Predicting the future is the toughest sport in creation. H.G. Wells, author of *The Time Machine,* is widely regarded as the Bart Starr of prognosticators, and yet, as Keith Olbermann might have said about him, he was forever drooling the drool of error into the pillow of miscalculation. During World War II, for instance, Wells prophesied that, if Europe managed to survive the slaughter, its civilizations would quickly unravel into primitivism. Europeans, he wrote sadly, would become ever more mired in petty nationalist disputes, separating into bands of hostile tribes and battling one another with rudimentary weapons—rather like the Middle Ages, or *Mad Max*: *Beyond Thunderdome.* Baseball fans often marvel that a good hitter fails 70 percent of the time; a would-be prophet should be so lucky.

And yet, predicting the future is also one of the most fun sports in creation. College basketball pools, fantasy leagues, Off-Track Betting—all thrive because we sports lovers enjoy nothing more than the opportunity to show that we knew it would happen long before it did. In this spirit, the 25th anniversary of ESPN cries out for 25 predictions about the network's next 25 years. How will its highlights change? Will there be more women's sports, more X-treme sports, more X-rated sports, or more sports involving battling robots? What will be the catchphrases, hairstyles and neckties of the next quarter century? Et cetera, ad nauseam.

But the present writer, not half so prescient, or self-confident, as H.G. Wells, is too much of a coward to make 25 predictions about anything under the sun. Though accustomed to being wrong, I have never yet risked being wrong 25 times, in a bound volume that could someday be used by my children, or the rest of my enemies, to prove that I am a nincompoop. Let us be reasonable about this, and move the decimal over to the left just a tick. Here are 2.5 predictions about highlights—that is, two you can take to the bank and one wild speculation you wouldn't want to take anywhere.

First prediction: The highlight revolution has barely begun; in coming decades, sports fans will have access to literally thousands each day. The reason: digital technology. As of this writing, ESPN has invested millions in a state-of-the-art digital recording and editing system, and a cavernous new building in Bristol to house it. Perhaps you are thinking: So what? Well, I don't blame you. In recent years, everything from Duncan Hines recipe cards to the Strategic Air Command control system has been digitized (which, in

Perfect couple Swedish golfer Annika Sorenstam teams with Tiger Woods, a self-described "Cablinasian"—that is, of African, caucasian, Native American and Asian descent. As athletes continue to roll over the arbitrary barriers of race and sex, the face of ESPN will continue to change.

case you didn't know, simply means that it can be digested, and regurgitated, by a computer) . . . and yet, our life can still seem nasty, brutish and short.

Cheer up. In the short run, digital technology will improve the quality of the highlights you see on *SportsCenter*, just by rendering the technical process of making them less cumbersome. But in the titillating long run, this technology should someday allow you to watch highlights of just about anything, whenever you choose (for a price, of course), using your computer keyboard, or your TV remote, or your cell phone, or some other gizmo that hasn't been invented yet. Indeed, I venture to predict that every incident that occurs on any high-profile playing field will be reviewable by any fan, from numerous angles. It may sound like pie in the skybox, but the fact is, luxury seats in several sports venues have already been wired with touch-screens that allow wealthy fans (or just lucky ones) to view such replays during games and to access real-time stats and other minutiae that only a sports junkie could love. Our future is one in which fantasy leaguers, sports gamblers and celebrity stalkers will be able to ruminate over athletes almost indefinitely. Those of us with actual lives will benefit, too.

A second prediction: Highlights will become much more diverse—in every sense of the word, but especially the social sense. Professional sports are already so cosmopolitan that it's not even worth mentioning when the New York Yankees Japanese clean-up hitter stands in against the Boston Red Sox Dominican ace, or when the Houston Rockets superstar from China posts up the Dallas Mavericks superstar from Germany. As sports takes on an increasingly global character, so will ESPN. Indeed, someday your *SportsCenter* anchor may have as thick a foreign accent as Governor Schwarzenegger.

Believe it or not, this is probably something to look forward to. Going, and soon to be gone, are the days when a sportscaster is required to "look like a sportscaster"—that is, like a handsome male Caucasian in a pastel-colored sports coat, with a network logo emblazoned just above his left nipple. The traditional network sportscaster spoke with no detectable accent, and if he ever told a joke, he did it while his mike was turned off and you were in the bathroom. There's nothing wrong with that style of sportscasting, but it ought not be the viewing public's only choice. "Age, sex, race—all of these things factor into how you interpret something, and how you present it," says Dan Patrick. Logic dictates that a healthy mixture of ages, sexes, races and nationalities will yield a broader, richer experience for everyone.

Over the last 25 years, ESPN's doors have creaked open to admit more different types of people. What's encouraging is that the network has permitted at least some of those people the latitude to express themselves, differences and all. Stuart Scott is a case in point. Among his innovations is the "*SportsCenter* Def Poetry Jam," a feature in which he renders highlights entirely in rhyme. For instance, an emotional Duke basketball victory over rival North Carolina, led by guard Jason Williams, concluded thus:

> The day
> —like so many—
> belonged to Jay:
> 37 points, *his* way.
> Eleventh 30-point game of his career,
>   leaving a tear
>   in his eyes—
>   and in Coach K's eyes.
>   No surprise:
>   Duke glides.

Some may not care for this sort of thing, but it nonetheless shows that def poetry is a perfectly effective way of delivering sports news—which suggests that there must be many, many others beyond Let's go to the videotape! "A lot of people have come to see me as 'the hip-hop anchor,' but that's just a label," says Scott. "Hip-hop is part of who I am, but I never consciously set out to do anything in particular. What I love about ESPN is this: If you know your sports, and bust your tail and prove it every night, there's room for all kinds of diversity, all kinds of innovation." And, incidentally, a more inclusive public conversation about sports is likely to generate a much bigger global market, leading to more potential profits, and more money-driven sports hype and . . . and so on.

If all of this proves true—if highlights are destined to become exponentially

Roll your own highlight *Touchscreens at New York's Madison Square Garden allow fans to view replays from a dozen angles. Digital technology should one day allow you to do far more without leaving your sofa.*

more plentiful and accessible and pervasive—maybe they really will take over the world someday. Maybe new sports will be invented, or old ones redesigned, just to make the highlights more exciting and dramatic. Not a very appetizing prospect . . . but then, neither was the designated hitter. And with athletic celebrities popping up in every facet of American life, taking their seats on the boards of conglomerates and getting themselves elected to public office, sports has never had a greater influence over American life than it does today. This influence will grow, by leaps and bounds and 360-degree slams.

In February 2003, President George W. Bush casually remarked: "I don't spend too much time watching the national news. I get stuck with ESPN." Doubtless, the president was joshing—about missing the news, not about watching *SportsCenter*. For even as Mr. Bush prepared to lead his country into war with Iraq, *The New York Times* reported that the one-time part-owner of the Texas Rangers relaxed "by watching ESPN over lunch on a tray brought up to his private dining room from the White House mess."

Not even Bill Rasmussen could have imagined that the little cable TV enterprise he started would one day divert world leaders in times of international crisis. And yet, gargantuan as it has become, ESPN is still a child—and what's more, a child due for one hell of a growth spurt.

I advise you to stay tuned. The highlights should be outrageous. ∎

TIMELESS SPORTS ARGUMENTS

Thanks to the Internet, talk radio, sports bars and the explosion of "insider" information, we argue about sports more now than ever. Lots of the talk is about who's a better team or a better player, speculation that's almost always settled when a season, or a career, ends.

Other discussions are momentarily interesting, but are quickly shoveled into the dustbin of sports history. Should Piazza be traded? Who had the better TD celebration, Terrell Owens doing the Sharpie, or Joe Horn with his cell phone? Fun stuff, but we let it go easily.

The ones we list here are the "evergreens"—the topics that come up year after year, decade after decade, and never seem to be resolved. Pete Rose has managed to keep his name in the news for 15 years, even though he's been nothing more than a spectator since being tossed from baseball for gambling. Performance-enhancing drugs have been around since, probably, the ancient Greeks, and we'll be talking about them for a long time into the future.

Walk into a sports bar and mention any of the topics below—no matter what sport is in season. You're sure to be embroiled in a passionate—and usually well-informed—argument almost immediately. Two things are then guaranteed: You'll have a bunch of new friends, and you won't resolve anything.

1. Should Pete Rose be in the Hall of Fame?

Yes: No matter what Rose did or didn't do, he has the all-time hits record, for chrissake! And there are lots of questionable characters in the Hall. Ban him from the game, but let him in the Fame.

No: He committed the one cardinal sin of baseball, and deserves to be fully excommunicated.

2. Are the players juiced?

Yes: You don't gain 20 pounds of muscle mass in three months just by lifting weights. Most of today's hulking pros are taking illegal substances, and even negative tests are suspect, because it's easy to avoid detection.

No: Well, of course, some of them are. But most players are aware of the dangers of steroids and other performance-enhancing drugs and avoid them. Testing, as in the NFL, has also been a deterrent. Bigger, stronger, faster—that's natural improvement, enhanced by improved training methods.

3. Should college players in "revenue sports" be paid?

Yes: The schools make big bucks from basketball and football, while the players starve. It's not right. Paying players would reduce the temptation for taking money under the table, and would also acknowledge that most Division 1 athletes are there for sports, not for an education.

No: Isn't a scholarship enough? Let's keep the illusion of purity alive.

4. The BCS (Bowl Championship Series): Good or bad?

Good: Better than the politically influenced coaches and media polls, the entire setup gives us a very good idea of which college football team is the best.

Bad: Better than the old system? Maybe. But the old system was horrible; the BCS is merely terrible. The champ should be determined through a playoff system.

5. Is revenue sharing necessary to make baseball more "fair"?

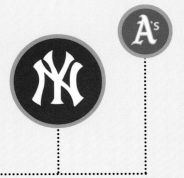

Yes: There's simply no way that small-market teams can compete against teams like the Yankees, Mets, Dodgers, Braves, Red Sox, etc. They've got the bucks and the huge media reach.

Too many fans of teams like the Royals know even before the season starts that their teams don't have a chance because they don't have the money for the big stars.

No: There's always been inequity in baseball, with teams mired in the second division for years or decades while other teams (like the Yankees) competed for the flag year after year. That didn't diminish the sport. Also, the A's, the Angels, the Twins and the Marlins have all demonstrated that you can field great teams on a low budget, while the Mets and Dodgers have shown you can field bad teams on a big budget.

6. Pro Athletes: Role models?

Yes: You can't get around it—kids look up to superstars and take cues on behavior (do's and don'ts) from them.

No: Barkley said it, and he's right: "I'm not a role model." It's a parent's job to teach children right from wrong. Athletes are entertainers, nothing more.

7. Should high schoolers be able to go straight to the pros?

Yes: High schoolers have been going pro straight from high school in baseball and hockey forever, and it works out just fine. An adult is an adult. If you're old enough to vote, get married, do everything else on your own, you should be able to go pro, no question. That doesn't mean it's necessarily a good thing to do, but look at how Kobe Bryant and Robin Yount flourished, even though they made it to the big time in their teens.

No: Just because it's possible and legally legit doesn't mean it's good. The pro leagues should take it upon themselves to set age limits and stick to them. There are too many pressures—psychological, physical, financial—for teens to go straight to the pros. Too many ruined careers.

8. Instant replay: Good or bad?

Good: Umps and refs are human. They make mistakes. No team should win on a bad call (unless it's my team).

Bad: Umps and refs are human. Players are human. Sports are human. Let's keep technology out of this—bad calls tend to even out, anyway.

9. Bobby Knight: Saint or sinner?

Saint: Knight is old-school and teaches his players to work hard, go to class, respect their elders and respect the game. He did more for Indiana than any professor, college president or governor. The guy's got a temper, but it's just because he won't take any guff.

Sinner: Knight's been a borderline psychotic for decades, and the only reason he hadn't been called on it is because he won titles. Knight's a serial physical abuser, and that's just way, way over the line. Indiana is better off without him.

10. Can a gay pro athlete openly state he's gay and still be accepted?

Yes: It's the last great barrier in sports, and although lots of athletes say they'd be uncomfortable around a gay teammate, most of them would eventually be accepting. Especially if the first guy to come out is a superstar.

No: Sports locker rooms are hypercharged hormonal hotbeds, among the last bastions of old-school machismo. No way a guy who's out will be accepted in that atmosphere, and the psychological stress would be impossible to endure.

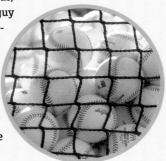

11. Is the ball juiced?

Yes: How could it not be? Take a look at the scores. And the dingers.

No: Scientific tests (and baseball's head honchos) say the ball's the same.

12. Are players overpaid?

Yes: You gotta be kidding me. Kids making millions for playing games, while teachers and firemen struggle to make ends meet? It's ridiculous.

No: This is capitalism, buddy. The players get exactly what they deserve, which is a lot of money, for sure. Would you prefer that the owners keep it?

13. Barry Bonds: Best hitter ever?

Yes: Look at the numbers. Babe Ruth is the only one who's his peer in that department, and he was playing at a time when there simply wasn't as much tough competition. And look at the fear Bonds inspires. Bonds dominates individual ballgames in a way Ruth never did.

No: Bonds is playing in an era of offense, against watered-down pitching. He's got better equipment, better training, and a whole lot of body armor, not to mention: BALCO. Give Ruth those advantages, and he'd put Bonds to shame.

14. Native American team names (Redskins, Braves, Fighting Sioux, etc.) Acceptable or offensive?

Acceptable: Most team names are long-standing and have a tradition all their own. They were intended to honor, not offend. Do we have to change anything that anyone finds offensive?

Offensive: Lots of team names are racist, plain and simple, and they've inspired slogans and fight songs that are similarly racist. Sports should be a big tent—why offend anyone when you can simply change the team name?

15. Phil Jackson: Greatest basketball coach ever?

Yes: He's had the respect of his players and won nine championships with two teams. There probably won't be another NBA coach who comes close to that record.

No: Give me MJ, then give me Shaq and Kobe. It's not that hard to win titles when you have the best players.

16. Should public prayer be allowed before high school games?

Yes: It may be public, but it's still optional. Those who don't want to pray don't have to. But most people want to.

No: It's not optional when everyone is doing it, and you're a teenager susceptible to peer pressure. And haven't you heard of the separation of church and state?

17. Should women be allowed to compete in men's sports?

Yes: If they're good enough, why not? The yardstick is ability, not gender. Suzy Whaley was the toast of the previously all-male Hartford Open in 2003.

No: Women have their own leagues and tours because, in general, they're not nearly as good as men in almost every sport. They're smaller, weaker, slower. And if women are allowed to play in men's sports, shouldn't men be allowed to play in women's leagues and tours?

18. Does Casey Martin (or any other athlete with a similar disability) have the right to a cart on the PGA tour?

Yes: To quote Martin himself, "I've never heard a competitor saying, 'Tiger is so great. Look at him walk.' It's not part of the game."

No: Have you ever walked five miles in hot weather? It makes you tired. If Casey rides and everyone else walks, he has an advantage. Also: Where does accommodating the disabled athletes stop? It's a slippery slope.

—Jeff Merron

ACKNOWLEDGEMENTS

IF YOU DON'T LIKE THIS BOOK, PLEASE DO NOT BLAME THE FOLLOWING: Jay Lovinger, mentor and mensch, who edited it; Hali Helfgott and Gueorgui Milkov, gifted young journalists, who contributed much valuable research; Craig Winston, Editorial Research Director at *ESPN The Magazine*, who provided every other resource a writer could possibly require.

I would also like to thank the following folks for answering many, many, many questions, without losing their tempers: John Anderson, Prof. Vernon Andrews, Prof. William J. Baker, Chris Berman, Shea Byram, Prof. Paul Christesen, Lynda Cohn, Rece Davis, Brian Downing, John Farmer, Dean Raymond Fielding, Grace Gallo, Alison Garber, Bill Graff, Wally Henry, Andy Hill, Michael Irvin, Tom Jackson, Prof. Martin Johnes, Trey Junkin, Suzy Kolber, Lee Leonard, Steve Levy, Bob Ley, Mark Malone, Coach Phil Martelli, Mo McMeekin, Mike McQuade, George Michael, Davey Miller, Fred Muzzy, Daniel Okrent, Prof. Michael Oriard, Chuck Pagano, Dan Patrick, Tom Picard, Neal Pilson, Mark Preisler, Jonathan Punko, Prof. Benjamin Rader, Jesse Radford, Bob Rauscher, Tom Reilly, Harold Reynolds, Sean Salisbury, John Schippman, Jeff Schneider, Howie Schwab, Stuart Scott, Heather Seibel, Bill Shanahan, Dan Steir, Prof. James P. Steyer, Robert Sullivan, Coach Pat Summit, Eric Swanson, Andy "Rat" Tillman, Steve Vecchione, John Walsh, Bill Walton, Jeff Wheatley, Norby Williamson, Warner Wolf . . . and the Dalai Lama of Basketball, Coach John Wooden, for a gentle reminder of how the game of life is meant to be played from buzzer to buzzer.

Extra special thanks to Barry Sacks, Mark Summer and Paul Dunn, three hyper-busy professionals who put up with two months of interruptions and irritating requests. And to the List Master, Jeff Merron.

I would also like to thank The Writers Room, a New York City writers' colony, for providing peace and quiet and many gallons of green tea.

Apologies to Gay Daly and Woo and Wendy Lovinger, for imperiling the unpredictable health of their husband and father, respectively.

Mountains of love and gratitude to my wife, Annette Foglino, whose favorite sport is yoga, but who nonetheless pretended to be enthusiastic about this project.

PICTURE CREDITS

Cover
First row, from left:
Rick LaBranche/ESPN,
Robert Beck/Sports Illustrated,
AP/Wide World Photos,
Tony Tomsic/SportsChrome,
Bettmann/Corbis.
Second row, from left:
Jed Jacobsohn/Getty Images,
Brian Snyder/Reuters/Corbis,
Rob Tringali, Jr./SportsChrome,
Jonathan Daniel/Getty Images,
Jed Jacobsohn/Getty Images.
Third row, from left:
NBAE/Getty Images,
Rich Arden/ESPN,
Art Resource,
Alex Livesey/Getty Images,
Rich Arden/ESPN.
Fourth row, from left:
Rich Pilling/MLB Photos,
AP/Wide World Photos,
Corbis,
Rich Pilling/MLB Photos,
AP/Wide World Photos.
Fifth row, from left:
Heinz Kluetmeier/Sports Illustrated,
David Liam Kyle/Sports Illustrated,
Republished with permission of Globe
Newspaper Company, Inc.,
Jonathan Daniel/Getty Images,
ESPN.

Dedication: Courtesy Charles Hirshberg
6-7: Jerry Wachter/Sports Illustrated (8)
9: ESPN (5)
10: Mark Cowan/Icon SMI (top), MLB Photos
13: Clockwise from top left: Robert Beck/
Sports Illustrated, Phil Huber, MLB Photos,
Jed Jacobsohn/Getty Images
14-15: Bridgeman Art Library
17: Art Resource
18: AP/Wide World Photos
19: Culver Pictures
20: Art Resource
21: Neil Leifer
22: Culver Pictures
24: Princeton University Library
26-27: Top, from left: AP/Wide World Photos
(3), Walter Iooss, Jr./NBAE/Getty Images,
Pacers Sports & Entertainment. Middle Row,
from left: AP/Wide World Photos, Wallace
Kirkland/Time-Life Pictures/Getty Images,
Jed Jacobsohn/Getty Images, Robert Landau/
Corbis, Chris Stanford/Getty Images,
Rich Clarkson Associates.
Bottom, from left: AP/Wide World Photos,
Jonathan Daniel/Getty Images, Rob Tringali,
Jr./SportsChrome, Frank DiBrango, John
Iacono/Sports Illustrated, David Eulitt
28: Clockwise from left: T.G. Higgins/Getty
Images, Rob Tringali, Jr./SportsChrome,
AP/Wide World Photos, Rick Stewart/Getty
Images, Jamie Squire/Getty Images, Rick
Stewart/Getty Images
29: HarpWeek
30-31: The Granger Collection
32-33: Library of Congress
34: Clockwise, from top left: Ken Levine/
Getty Images, Allen Steele/Getty Images,
Ken Levine/Getty Images, Eli Reichman,
Rick Stewart/Getty Images.
35: The Granger Collection
37: Globe Photos
38: Culver Pictures
40: I.O.C./Getty Images
41-42: Leni Riefenstahl Productions
43: Globe Photos
44-45: First row, from left: John Iacono/
Sports Illustrated, V.J. Lovero/Sports
Illustrated, Courtesy Boston University,

Rob Tringali, Jr./SportsChrome, Courtesy
David Trosso/Baltimore Ravens. Second row,
from left: Garrett Ellwood/Getty Images,
Kin Man Hui/San Antonio Express News,
Courtesy Cleveland Browns, Stephen
Dunn/Getty Images, Steve Woltman/
SportsChrome. Third row from left:
Rob Tringali, Jr./SportsChrome, Al Tielemans/
Sports Illustrated, Courtesy Jacksonville
Jaguars, Steve Woltman/ SportsChrome,
Courtesy University of Tennessee, Greg Crisp/
SportsChrome, Fourth Row, from left:
Gerry Thomas, Courtesy University of
Delaware, Courtesy University of California -
Santa Cruz, Barry Gossage/Getty Images,
AP/Wide World Photos, Doug Pensinger/
Getty Images.
47: AP/Wide World Photos (top),
ABC Photo Archive
49: NFL Properties
51: NFL Properties (top), Photofest
52-53: ESPN
54: George Long/Sports Illustrated
55-58: ESPN
59: AP/Wide World Photos (3)
60-61: Photofest
62-63: ESPN
64: From top: AFP/Getty Images, Getty
Images, Bettmann/Corbis
65: From top: Mike Segar/Reuters/Corbis,
Bettmann/Corbis,
AFP/Getty Images (2)
66: Corbis
68-69: Ronald C. Modra/Sports Illustrated
(top), AP/Wide World Photos
70: Paul A. Souders/Corbis
71: ESPN
72: AP/Wide World Photos (top),
Jonathan Ferrey/Getty Images
73: NFL Properties (top), Reuters/Corbis
74-75: Top, from left: Rob Tringali, Jr./
SportsChrome, John Zich/NewSport/Corbis,
AFP/Getty Images, Michael Zagaris/MLB
Photos, Bettmann/Corbis, AP/Wide World
Photos. Middle, from left: Corbis, AP/Wide
World Photos (2), Tom Dipace/SportsChrome,
Tony Tomsic/SportsChrome (2), Rich Pilling/
MLB Photos, Jonathan Daniel/Getty Images.

Bottom,from left: Elsa/Getty Images,
Jonathan Ferrey/Getty Images,
John F. Grieshop/Sports Illustrated,
Chris Livingston/ Getty Images, Otto Greule,
Jr./Getty Images, Jonathan Daniel/
Getty Images.
76-77: AP/Wide World Photos
78: Photofest
79: Jonathan Daniel/Getty Images
80-81: First row, from left:
TempSport/Corbis, AP/Wide World Photos,
Rebecca Cook/Reuters/Corbis, Linda Spillers/
ESPN, AP/Wide World Photos (2),
Colin Braley/Reuters/Corbis. Second row,
from left: Rob Tringali Jr./SportsChrome,
AFP/Getty Images, AP/Wide World Photos(3),
Justin Kase Conder/Icon SMI, Robert
Beck/Sports Illustrated. Third row, from left:
AP/Wide World Photos, Ronald Martinez/
Getty Images, Clive Brunskill/Getty Images,
AFP/Getty Images, Bill Greenblatt/
UPI/Corbis, Tim DeFrisco/Getty Images,
AP/Wide World Photos, AFP/Getty Images.
Fourth row, from left: AP/Wide World Photos,
John Cordes/Sporting News/Icon SMI, S.
Carmona/Corbis, Jonathan Daniel/Getty
Images, Desmond Boylan/Reuters/Corbis,
AP/Wide World Photos, John Biever/Sports
Illustrated, AP/Wide World Photos.
Fifth row, from left: Reuters/Corbis,
AFP/Getty Images, Jed Jacobsohn/Getty
Images, Chris Trotman/ Getty Images,
NBAE/Getty Images, AP Wide World Photos,
NBAE/Getty Images, Sue Ogrocki/
Reuters/Corbis.
83: From left: AP/Wide World Photos,
Ron Modra/Sports Illustrated,
Heinz Kluetmeier/Sports Illustrated
84: Heinz Kluetmeier/Sports Illustrated
(center), Ronald C. Modra/Sports Illustrated (2)
86-87: Manny Millan/Sports Illustrated
89: From top: Reuters/Corbis, Jerry Wachter/
Sports Illustrated, Jose M. Osorio/
Sacramento Bee
90: From top: AP/Wide World Photos,
Jamie Squire/Getty Images, Reuters/Corbis
91: AP/Wide World Photos
92: Jonathan Daniel/Getty Images

93: From left: Sports Illustrated, V.J. Lovero/
Icon SMI, Ron Wyatt/SportsChrome, Courtesy
Toronto Blue Jays
95: AP/Wide World Photos
96: Clockwise from top: David Liam Kyle/
Sports Illustrated, AP/Wide World Photos,
Courtesy Chicago Cubs
97: From left: Express Syndication/Getty
Images, AP/Wide World Photos,
Robert Rogers/Sports Illustrated
99: Nike
100-101: ESPN
103: Rick LaBranche/ESPN
104-105: Top, from left: John B. Zissel/
IPOL/Globe Photos, Alex Livesey/Getty
Images, David Wahlberg/Sports Illustrated,
Michael Caulfield/Wireimage, Mychal Watts/
Wireimage, Kevin Mazur/Wireimage. Bottom,
from left: George Lange/Corbis Outline,
Lorenzo Agius/Corbis Outline, Catherine
Wessel/Corbis Outline, Stephane Cardinale/
Corbis, Michael O'Neill/Corbis Outline.
106: Rick Stewart/Getty Images
107: James V. Biever (top),
AP/Wide World Photos
108: Icon SMI
109: Clockwise, from top right: Rich Pilling/
NBAE/Getty Images, AP/Wide World Photos,
Rich Pilling/MLB Photos, A.J. Mast/
Icon SMI (2)
110-111: From left: AP/Wide World Photos
(3), David Wahlberg/Sports Illustrated
112: AP/Wide World Photos
114-115: Republished with permission of
Globe Newspaper Company, Inc.
116: Getty Images
118-119: Tina Buckman
120: Icon SMI
121: Bettmann/Corbis
122: AP/Wide World Photos (top),
Tim DeFrisco/Getty Images
123: Rick Stewart/Getty Images (top),
Peter Read Miller/Sports Illustrated
124: Stephen Dunn/Getty Images (top),
AFP/Getty Images
125: Anthony Neste/Sports Illustrated
127: Alan Hawes/The Post & Courier
129: Mike Blake/Reuters/Corbis

131: Joe McNally
132: Rich Pilling/MLB Photos
133: Ezra Shaw/Getty Images (top)
134: Barry Gutierrez-Pool/Getty Images
(top), NBAE/Getty Images
135: From top: Doug Pensinger/Getty Images,
Mark Lyons/Getty Images, Jeff Gross/
Getty Images
136: Jonathan Daniel/Getty Images (top),
Brian Bahr/Getty Images
137: From top: NBAE/Getty Images, Getty
Images, Scott Halleran/Getty Images